A SANCTUARY OF ZEUS
ON
MOUNT HYMETTOS

BY

MERLE K. LANGDON

AMERICAN SCHOOL OF CLASSICAL STUDIES AT ATHENS
PRINCETON, NEW JERSEY
1976

Library of Congress Cataloging in Publication Data

Langdon, Merle K   1945-
   A sanctuary of Zeus on Mount Hymettos.

   (Hesperia : Supplement ; 16)
   Includes index.
   1. Hymettus Mountain, Greece—Antiquities.
2. Excavations (Archaeology)—Greece—Hymettus Mountain. 3. Inscriptions, Greek—Hymettus Mountain,
Greece. 4. Zeus. I. Title. II. Series: Hesperia,
journal of the American School of Classical Studies
at Athens : Supplement ; 16.
DF221.H94L36   938'.5   76-16777
ISBN 0-87661-516-7

IN MEMORIAM

RODNEY S. YOUNG

AUGUST 1, 1907—OCTOBER 25, 1974

PREFACE

The mountain tops of Greece have not frequently been the subject of serious archaeological study. Ancient military installations located on mountain peaks have received a fair amount of attention, but other types of sites have as often as not gone unnoticed or ignored. It is in large part the object of the present work to rectify this situation for one area of Greece.

My study of mountain-top sites in Attica centers around an excavated but incompletely published site on the summit of Mount Hymettos. The results were presented as a doctoral dissertation to the Department of Classical Archaeology of the University of Pennsylvania in 1972, and the present work is an expanded version of that study.

Research which touches on such a wide variety of topics—excavation material widely ranging in date and kind, topographic matters, ancient Greek religion and history—cannot be adequately pursued by one person without help and guidance. I acknowledge with great pleasure the aid which I received from a large number of scholars. Although they are too numerous to all receive mention here, some of those who advised me must be named. Michael H. Jameson read most of the manuscript and made improvements practically everywhere. Eugene Vanderpool contributed his special gifts and talents in ways too numerous to list. Lilian H. Jeffery made valuable suggestions concerning the Archaic graffiti. Elizabeth W. French, Evelyn L. Smithson, Keith de Vries, and Judith Perlzweig Binder all saved me from errors in the section on pottery. I also profited from discussions with Homer A. Thompson, Alison Frantz, and Jeremy Rutter. Points of disagreement remain, and it would be in poor appreciation of their help if I failed to stress that these scholars are not in any way to be implicated in my opinions, or errors which remain.

I wish to thank James R. McCredie, Director of the American School of Classical Studies at Athens, for obtaining for me some necessary study permits. I am grateful to T. Leslie Shear, Jr., Director of the Agora Excavations, and his staff, especially Poly Demoulini, then secretary, Eugene Vanderpool, Jr., and Spiro Spyropoulos, for facilitating my study of Hymettos material stored in the Stoa of Attalos, and to Barbara Philippaki of the National Museum in Athens for like kindness regarding the Hymettos material stored there.

My deep gratitude must also go to the Publications Committee of the American School of Classical Studies for undertaking the publication of this study. It was a real pleasure to work with the editor, Marian H. McAllister, in whose capable hands the manuscript acquired acceptable shape for publication.

The site plans were drawn by Dorothy Cox in 1939. The graffiti, except for **1**, were drawn by Hazel Whipple. **1** was drawn by Helen Besi. The photographs of material in the National Museum were taken by Hermann Wagner. The other photographs are mine.

In conclusion, I must record my profound regret that the manuscript of this publication was not submitted in time to be produced for the cognizant hands of the two men who excavated and first studied the site on Mount Hymettos. Carl W. Blegen had long since relinquished control of any of the material, but he followed my work with interest and encouragement. Rodney S. Young entrusted to me for study and publication all of the excavated material. He provided me with much help, and he maintained an active interest in the progress of my work until his tragic death in October 1974. It is in his memory that this study is respectfully dedicated.

MERLE K. LANGDON

ATHENS
MARCH 4, 1975

TABLE OF CONTENTS

ABBREVIATIONS AND SELECTED BIBLIOGRAPHY

A.A.A. = *Athens Annals of Archaeology*

Agora = *The Athenian Agora, Results of Excavations Conducted by the American School of Classical Studies at Athens*

    IV: R. H. Howland, *Greek Lamps and Their Survivals*, Princeton, 1958.

    V: H. S. Robinson, *Pottery of the Roman Period, Chronology*, Princeton, 1959.

    VII: J. Perlzweig, *Lamps of the Roman Period, First to Seventh Century after Christ*, Princeton, 1961.

    VIII: E. Brann, *Late Geometric and Protoattic Pottery, Mid 8th to Late 7th Century B.C.*, Princeton, 1961.

    XII: B. Sparkes and L. Talcott, *Black and Plain Pottery of the 6th, 5th, and 4th Centuries B.C.*, Princeton, 1972.

A.J.A. = *American Journal of Archaeology.*

A.J.P. = *American Journal of Philology.*

Arch. Anz. = *Jahrbuch des deutschen Instituts, Archäologische Anzeiger.*

Arch. Class. = *Archaeologia Classica.*

Ἀρχ. Ἐφ. = Ἀρχαιολογικὴ Ἐφημερίς.

Ath. Mitt. = *Mitteilungen des deutschen archäologischen Instituts. Athenische Abteilung.*

B.C.H. = *Bulletin de correspondance hellénique.*

B.S.A. = *The Annual of the British School at Athens.*

Blegen, C. W., "Inscriptions on Geometric Pottery from Hymettos," *A.J.A.* 38, 1934, pp. 10-28.

Brann. Catalogue references prefixed:

    E-H or S = E. Brann, "Protoattic Well Groups from the Athenian Agora," *Hesperia* 30, 1961, pp. 305-379.

    I-R = E. Brann, "Late Geometric Well Groups from the Athenian Agora," *Hesperia* 30, 1961, pp. 93-146.

    Catalogue numbers:

    1-659 = E. Brann, *The Athenian Agora*, VIII, *Late Geometric and Protoattic Pottery*, Princeton, 1962.

Brann, E., "Late Geometric Graves from the Athenian Agora," *Hesperia* 29, 1960, pp. 402-416.

Bull. Metr. Mus. = *The Metropolitan Museum of Art Bulletin.*

C.W. = *Classical World.*

Carpenter, R., "The Greek Alphabet Again," *A.J.A.* 42, 1938, pp. 58-69.

Coldstream, *G.G.P.* = J. N. Coldstream, *Greek Geometric Pottery*, London, 1968.

Cook, *Zeus* = A. B. Cook, *Zeus. A Study in Ancient Religion*, I-III, Cambridge, 1914-1940.

Corinth XIII = C. W. Blegen, H. Palmer, R. S. Young, *Corinth, Results of Excavations Conducted by the American School of Classical Studies at Athens*, XIII, *The North Cemetery*, Princeton, 1964.

Day, J., *An Economic History of Athens under Roman Domination*, New York, 1942.

Délos XV = C. Dugas and C. Rhomaios, *Exploration archéologique de Délos faite par l'École française d'Athènes*, XV, *Les vases préhélleniques et géométriques*, Paris, 1934.

Δελτ. = Ἀρχαιολογικὸν Δελτίον.

Desborough, *Protogeometric Pottery* = V. R. d'A. Desborough, *Protogeometric Pottery*, Oxford, 1952.

Deubner, L., *Attische Feste*, Berlin, 1932.

Ἐφ. Ἀρχ. See Ἀρχ. Ἐφ.

Frazer, *Pausanias* = J. G. Frazer, *Pausanias's Description of Greece*, I-VI, London, 1898.

Furtwängler, A., *Aegina, Das Heiligtum der Aphaia*, Munich, 1906.

Geagan, D. J., *Hesperia*, Suppl. XII, *The Athenian Constitution after Sulla*, Princeton, 1967.

Guarducci, M., "Appunti di epigrafia greca arcaica," *Arch. Class.* 16, 1964, pp. 122-153.

————, *Epigrafia Greca I*, Rome, 1967.

Heichelheim, F., " Sitos," *R.E.*, Suppl. VI, cols. 819-892.

Howe, T. P., " Linear B and Hesiod's Breadwinners," *T.A.P.A.* 89, 1958, pp. 44-65.

J.H.S = *Journal of Hellenic Studies*.

Jeffery, *L.S.A.G.* = L. H. Jeffery, *The Local Scripts of Archaic Greece*, Oxford, 1961.

Kerameikos IV = K. Kübler, *Kerameikos, Ergebnisse der Ausgrabungen. Neufunde aus der Nekropole des 11. und 10. Jahrhunderts*, Berlin, 1943.

Kerameikos V, 1 = K. Kübler, *Kerameikos, Ergebnisse der Ausgrabungen der Nekropole des 10. bis 8. Jahrhunderts*, Berlin, 1954.

Kerameikos VI, 2 = K. Kübler, *Kerameikos, Ergebnisse der Ausgrabungen. Die Nekropole des späten 8. bis frühen 6. Jahrhunderts*, Berlin, 1970.

Kotzias, N., ⟨⟨Ἀνασκαφὴ ἐν Προφήτῃ Ἠλίᾳ Ὑμηττοῦ⟩⟩, Πρακτικά, 1949, pp. 51-74.

————, ⟨⟨Ἀνασκαφαὶ ἐν Προφήτῃ Ἠλίᾳ Ὑμηττοῦ⟩⟩, Πρακτικά, 1950, pp. 144-172.

Kourouniotis, K., ⟨⟨Ἀνασκαφαὶ Λυκαίου⟩⟩, Ἀρχ. Ἐφ., 1904, cols. 153-214.

Lehmann, K., *Samothrace 2*, II, *The Inscriptions on Ceramics and Minor Objects*, New York, 1960.

McCredie, *Fortified Camps* = J. R. McCredie, *Hesperia*, Suppl. XI, *Fortified Military Camps in Attica*, Princeton, 1966.

A. Milchhöfer, *Text* = A. Milchhöfer, *Erläuternder Text* to E. Curtius and J. A. Kaupert, *Karten von Attika*, Berlin, 1881-1891.

Nilsson, M., *Greek Popular Religion*, New York, 1940.

————, *Geschichte der griechischen Religion*, 3rd ed., Munich, 1967.

Payne, H., *Necrocorinthia, a Study of Corinthian Art in the Archaic Period*, Oxford, 1931.

Payne, H. and others, *Perachora, The Sanctuaries of Hera Akraia and Limenia, Architecture, Bronzes, Terracottas, Excavations of the British School of Archaeology at Athens*, Oxford, 1940.

Perachora II = T. J. Dunbabin and others, *Perachora, The Sanctuaries of Hera Akraia and Limenia, Excavations of the British School of Archaeology at Athens, 1930-1933*, II, *Pottery, Ivories, Scarabs, and Other Objects from the Votive Deposit of Hera Limenia*, Oxford, 1962.

Perlzweig = J. Perlzweig, *The Athenian Agora*, VII, *Lamps of the Roman Period*, Princeton, 1961.

Popham, M. R. and Sackett, L. H., *Excavations at Lefkandi, Euboea: 1964-66*, London, 1968.

Πρακτικά = Πρακτικὰ τῆς ἐν Ἀθήναις Ἀρχαιολογικῆς Ἑταιρείας.

S.E.G. = *Supplementum Epigraphicum Graecum*.

Smithson, E. L., " The Tomb of a Rich Athenian Lady, *ca.* 850 B.C.," *Hesperia* 37, 1968, pp. 77-116.

T.A.P.A. = *Transactions of the American Philological Association*.

Thorikos I-VI = H. F. Mussche and others, *Thorikos, Rapport préliminaire sur la première (deuxième*, etc.) *campagne de fouilles*, Brussels, 1968-1973.

Welter, G., "Aeginetica I-XII," *Arch. Anz.* 33, 1938, cols. 1-33.

Wrede, W., *Attika*, Athens, 1934.

Young (catalogue nos.) = R. S. Young, *Hesperia*, Suppl. II, *Late Geometric Graves and a Seventh Century Well in the Agora*, Athens, 1939.

Young, R. S., " Pottery from a Seventh Century Well," *Hesperia* 7, 1938, pp. 412-428.

————, " Excavations on Mount Hymettos, 1939," *A.J.A.* 44, 1940, pp. 1-9.

————, " Graves from the Phaleron Cemetery," *A.J.A.* 46, 1942, pp. 23-57.

Publication of this Supplement has been aided by gifts from:

THE ALUMNI ASSOCIATION OF THE AMERICAN SCHOOL OF CLASSICAL STUDIES
AT ATHENS

and

CONSTANCE C. BARHAM
CEDRIC G. and PATRICIA N. BOULTER
JOHN L. CASKEY
ELIZABETH G. CASKEY
ELSA GIBSON
CLAIRÈVE GRANDJOUAN
LOUISE A. HOLLAND
HENRY S. and SARA A. IMMERWAHR
VIRGINIA JAMESON

DONALD R. LAING, JR.
MABEL L. LANG
K. SHATTUCK MARVIN
LOUIS E. and MARIAN H. MCALLISTER
BENJAMIN D. and LUCY S. MERITT
ANTHONY and ISABEL RAUBITSCHEK
HOMER A. THOMPSON
EUGENE VANDERPOOL
HENRY YOUNG, JR.

CHAPTER I

THE SITE

LOCATION AND EXCAVATION

Investigations of a site near the summit of Mount Hymettos were conducted by Carl Blegen in 1923 and 1924 and by him and Rodney S. Young in 1939 and 1940.[1] The site centers around a natural depression or hollow located somewhat less than half a mile north of the highest point. The hollow is deep and well sheltered. From it one has no view but can see only its rocky sides and the sky (Pl. 2). From just above the depression, however, one enjoys an unobstructed view of the entire Athenian plain.[2] Eastern Attica, on the other hand, is completely cut off from view by the ridge which rises still higher east of the hollow. Today the entire summit is a restricted military zone, and the excavated depression has become the home of an Albanian refugee who is allowed to keep his pigs there.[3]

ARCHITECTURE

The crude foundations of three humble structures were uncovered during the excavations. R. S. Young gave the most plausible interpretation to the remains in his preliminary report. Two foundations found outside the hollow may have been enclosure walls with simple open-air altars within. The larger foundation (Fig. 1), approximately 5.80 meters on a side, lay above and just to the west of the hollow. It was built of rough stones loosely laid on bedrock, with no bonding material between them. The south and west walls were relatively narrow (ca. 0.80 m. thick) compared with the north and east walls (each 2.00 m. thick). Inside this enclosure some flat paving slabs were preserved in the southwest corner, and against the east wall was a pile of stones which may have been the remains of a rude altar. The smaller foundation (Fig. 2), 31 meters north of this, may have been a similar enclosure, although when found it preserved only two parallel sides, neither of which turned a corner at the ends. A curved foundation inside the hollow (Fig. 3), 2.80 meters in diameter, was perhaps a stone-lined storage pit for votives. The excavators were uncertain whether or not some stones immediately south of this pit

---

[1] For Young's preliminary account, and references to previous reports, see *A.J.A.* 44, 1940, pp. 1-9. Unfortunately, the site could not be completely investigated because of the war. Excavations closed down on October 28, 1940, and were never reopened.

[2] An interesting if fanciful description of the depression and view is given by V. Scully, *The Earth, the Temple, and the Gods,* New Haven and London, 1962, pp. 135-136.

[3] I was permitted by Greek military authorities to visit the site once, in April 1971.

FIG. 1. Plan of Altar of Zeus

belonged to another pit or chamber. Figure 4 shows the location of these foundations in relation to the hollow.[4]

IDENTIFICATION

The site is identified as a sanctuary of Zeus by the discovery of several sherds with inscribed dedications mentioning that deity by name.[5] Only one of them pre-

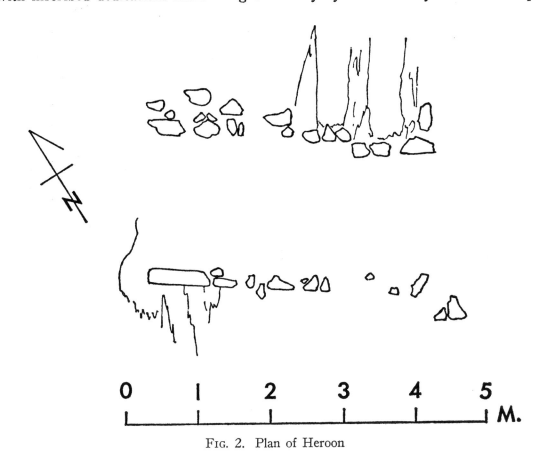

FIG. 2. Plan of Heroon

serves a title, a dedication to Zeus Semios, but the exact nature of the worship of Zeus here can be clarified by a consideration of other data relating to the mountain.

Throughout most of antiquity, and even into modern times, Hymettos was regarded as a natural weather indicator, especially for approaching rain.[6] A thick concentration of clouds massed along its summit was, and still is today, considered an

[4] Because of their flimsy construction the foundations have not withstood the passage of time. The two above the hollow were destroyed during construction of the asphalt road which serves the military installations on the summit, and the one inside the hollow has disappeared under a mass of trash and rubble.

[5] These are discussed more fully in Chapter II.

[6] See Theophrastos, *de Signis Tempestatum* 1, 20, 24; 3 43,

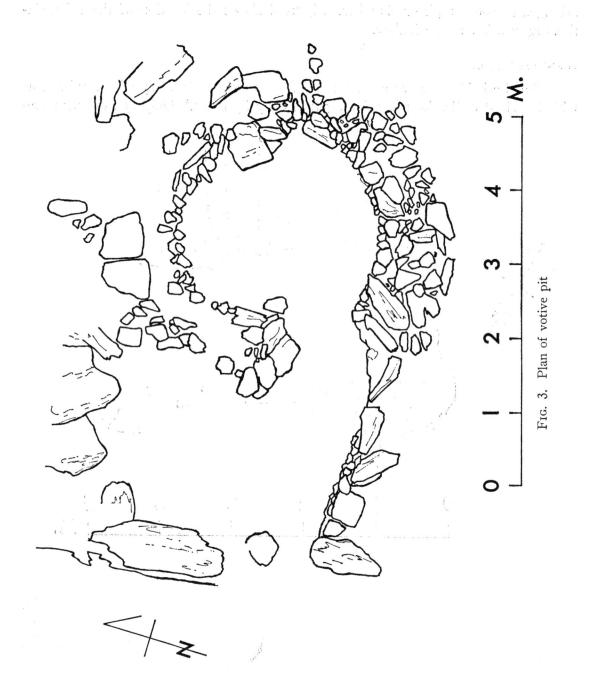

FIG. 3. Plan of votive pit

almost certain portent of impending showers. This property of the mountain was acknowledged in ancient times by the emplacement somewhere on its height of an altar of Zeus Ombrios (Showery Zeus).[7] It is not stated exactly where the altar was situated, but we might reasonably conjecture that it lay on the very top where the rain-prophetic qualities of the mountain and the rain god himself would form a most appropriate association. Indeed, I have no doubt that the altar of Zeus Ombrios mentioned by Pausanias was on the very summit of Hymettos, and since no other remains of a religious nature have been found there,[8] I believe that the site excavated by Blegen and Young is that same sacred spot.

The site of the altar of Zeus Ombrios has long been placed elsewhere. Milchhöfer, followed by Kolbe, located it on the east slope of Hymettos, on the height of Profitis Elias above Koropi.[9] Here, on a small, sloping plateau which commands a good view of the Mesogeia plain, there is a chapel of Elias built on an ancient foundation. Milchhöfer noted that the local population resorted to this chapel during periods of drought in order to offer prayers for rain. He concluded that in antiquity the place probably served a similar function and that the foundation under the chapel probably represented the altar of Zeus Ombrios.

The area was investigated later by the Greek archaeologist N. Kotzias, who showed that the foundation under the chapel actually belonged to a temple of the 6th century B.C. In his first preliminary report Kotzias followed Milchhöfer's line of reasoning and concluded that the temple belonged to Zeus Ombrios.[10] But after uncovering another, smaller temple a short distance to the west during subsequent excavations, he changed his mind and assigned Zeus Ombrios to the smaller one.[11] He was prompted to do this by the discovery at the smaller temple of an abundance of sherds belonging to the pointed-bottomed amphoras and hydrias, which he felt were suitable offerings for the rain god.[12] He also argued that since the temple went out of use long before the time of Pausanias, the periegete mentioned only an altar.

[7] Pausanias, I, 32, 2. There is no reason to think that Pausanias actually visited the site. He merely wrote down what he was told.

[8] The whole summit was thoroughly searched by Young, but he failed to find any other remains suggestive of religious activity. The same may be said for great numbers of students and scholars of the American School who for many years were in the habit of hiking all over the summit-ridge of Hymettos. Besides the excavated sanctuary the only other noteworthy ancient remains on the summit of Hymettos are two military structures, one a camp of uncertain date south of the main peak (J. R. McCredie, *Fortified Camps*, pp. 48-50), the other a watchtower of the late 5th to early 4th centuries B.C. on a height above Liopesi (*ibid.*, pp. 117-119).

[9] A. Milchhöfer, *Text* II, p. 32; W. Kolbe in *R.E., s.v.* Hymettos, col. 139.

[10] Πρακτικά, 1949, pp. 51-74.

[11] Πρακτικά, 1950, pp. 114-172.

[12] *Ibid.*, pp. 157-158. The results of the excavations are summarized by J. Boersma, *Athenian Building Policy from 561/0 to 405/4 B.C.*, Groningen, 1970, p. 200, no. 71. But Boersma apparently overlooked Kotzias' about-face on the identification of the temple of Zeus Ombrios, since he credits the archaeologist solely with the attribution to the sanctuary of Zeus of the foundation under the chapel.

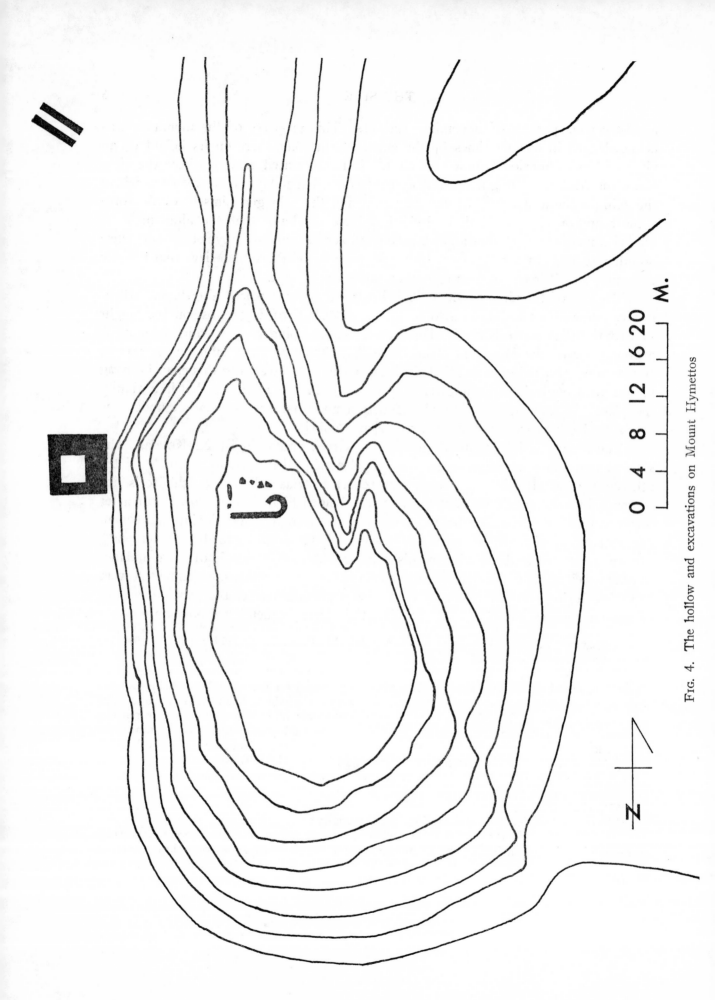

Fig. 4. The hollow and excavations on Mount Hymettos

But none of Kotzias' reasoning is cogent, and his conclusions cannot be taken seriously. It is true that Elias is the general heir-apparent of Zeus on mountain tops.[13] He is an important figure in the Greek Orthodox faith, the one to whom prayers are directed especially for rain, and his small chapels are a familiar sight crowning many peaks about the Greek countryside. In this case, however, the mere presence of a chapel of Profitis Elias built on a temple foundation is not good evidence for concluding that in antiquity Zeus Ombrios was worshipped nearby. Not a single dedication was found by Kotzias to indicate the deities worshipped in these two temples, and in view of the lack of evidence, we should refrain from further guesswork about them.

FUNCTION AND USE

The site near the summit of Mount Hymettos is definitely identified as a sanctuary of Zeus. The arguments presented above even allow the conclusion that it is the sanctuary of Zeus Ombrios. Admittedly this is still only a hypothesis, but it can be maintained with greater confidence than that of Kotzias. The ceramic material, which will be examined later, reveals that the altar on the summit was in use mainly from the 12th to the 6th centuries B.C. On the other hand, Pausanias gives us our earliest reference to the altar of Zeus Ombrios a number of centuries later. If in fact the two altars are one and the same, it is quite possible that the title Ombrios was not conferred upon the deity until later times, and that earlier on he was honored with whatever epithet each votary wished to use. The scanty epigraphical material cited above would seem to suggest this.

It will be argued below, however, that the great majority of offerings at all periods of use of the altar were brought to Zeus as offerings for rain. Anticipating this discussion a little, I should like to put forward the following tentative conclusions. The sanctuary of Zeus seems clearly to have served as a place to which the agricultural population could go seeking the favor of the rain god. It was probably founded and predominantly used by residents of the entire Athenian plain. We should not think of it as an exclusively Athenian sanctuary, even though Hymettos and Athens are closely connected, and the mountain does form a familiar and distinctive feature of the setting of the city. Clouds on Hymettos were visible and proclaimed rain to everyone alike, and the summit was easily approachable from other localities besides Athens. Also, the sanctuary flourished in the Geometric and early Archaic periods when Athens was a relatively small town, not much larger than other neighboring settlements. So the sanctuary must have served other inhabitants and communities in the Athenian plain as well.

The proper distinction to be drawn is that the sanctuary was used mainly by people living on the western side of Hymettos and not so much by those dwelling

[13] See the discussion in *Zeus* I, pp. 163-186.

to the east. Topographical circumstances in large part dictate this conclusion. From
the west the summit is quite easily reached by a number of approaches. Perhaps
the easiest route follows the long, wide backbone of rock which runs continuously
and directly to the top from just above Kaisariani monastery.[14] The east slope, in
contrast, is much steeper and offers no easy and direct route to the summit. There
is one good path from Paiania over a saddle, but it leads to Athens without passing
near the summit. Some inhabitants of the Mesogeia, especially those living close to
Hymettos, no doubt did struggle to the sanctuary to leave offerings, but they must not
have done so in very great numbers. Most of them instead visited sanctuaries located
on various mountains in eastern Attica (see Appendix B), thus leaving the Hymettos
sanctuary to the dwellers of the Athenian plain.

[14] Though the slope is not always gentle and there is no real path, one may pick his way quite
easily along this ridge. When the site was being excavated, the excavators climbed to the summit
each day this way, taking about an hour and a quarter on foot from Kaisariani.

CHAPTER II

THE GRAFFITI

Much work has been done to determine the date and place of formulation of the Greek alphabet. R. S. Young has recently presented new information for our understanding of the early Greek alphabet by publishing the Old Phrygian inscriptions found at Gordion.[1] Using this evidence Young has demonstrated that the common ancestral alphabet of both Greek and Phrygian must have been conceived during the first half of the 8th century B.C. somewhere on the Cilician or Levantine coast, and that its dissemination northward and westward must have begun around 750. L. H. Jeffery argues for similar dates in her study of the epichoric Greek scripts.[2]

Dates for the internal development of the Greek alphabet are less secure. A certain amount of early epigraphical material does exist, but there are enough large gaps to obscure our understanding of how writing spread in Greece during the late 8th and early 7th centuries B.C. Even for Attica, which boasts the largest number of extant early Greek inscriptions, we cannot state with confidence exactly when or from where the art of writing was introduced.

Judging from the material that is available, we may conclude that Athens was one of the first places on the western side of the Aigean to adopt alphabetical writing. The earliest inscription from Attica (and from all of Greece) is the hexameter verse scratched on the Dipylon oinochoe. This vessel was found in the Kerameikos cemetery and dates to *ca.* 740 B.C.[3] It thus stands alone almost half a century before the next examples of Attic writing. Because of its unique position, however, this inscription should be used as evidence for early Attic writing only with great caution. It has been argued that the jug's inscriber was not even an Athenian but rather a visitor from one of the early Greek-writing centers in the east.[4] In view of the

---

[1] *Hesperia* 38, 1969, pp. 252-296.

[2] *L.S.A.G.*, pp. 12-21. Any new discussion of the matter which fails to take into consideration the Phrygian evidence is at once invalidated. This may certainly be said of the latest attempt to put the origin of the Greek alphabet earlier: J. Naveh, *A.J.A.* 77, 1973, pp. 1-8. M. Guarducci, *Arch. Class.* 16, 1964, pp. 127-131, does consider the Phrygian evidence, but as she wrote before Young's full publication of the Phrygian inscriptions from Gordion, she misinterpreted the evidence in arguing for a date in the 9th century B.C. for the formulation of the Greek alphabet.

[3] This oinochoe has at various times been dated as early as the beginning of the 8th century and as late as the early 7th century. Now that our knowledge of Attic Geometric pottery is on a firmer basis, we may assign it with assurance to the Workshop of the Dipylon Master (*ca.* 740 B.C.): cf. Jean M. Davison, *Yale Class. Stud.* 16, 1961, p. 73, no. 3; Coldstream, *G.G.P.*, p. 32, no. 36, and pp. 358-359.

[4] Jeffery, *L.S.A.G.*, pp. 15-16; see also Young, *Hesperia,* Suppl. II, 1939, p. 229. For arguments that the inscription on the oinochoe was written by an Athenian, see Guarducci, *op. cit.* (note 2, above), pp. 134-136.

great differences between the script of the oinochoe and the next earliest inscriptions from Attica, the graffiti from Hymettos, this argument seems convincing. The complete absence of writing on the rest of Attic Geometric pottery adds further support to this belief.

Of the graffiti from Mount Hymettos the late Carl Blegen published twenty-two and R. S. Young twelve of the more complete fragments. An additional 165 inscribed pieces were recovered, both in excavating and in sorting through the dump. Most of these consist of but three or four preserved letters.[5] These graffiti constitute the largest body of early Attic inscriptions yet found, and their date is of prime importance.

The great majority of the inscribed sherds belong to simple types of one-handled cups (so-called Phaleron cups) and skyphoi which are deep in relation to their diameter and undecorated except for a hasty covering of dull, streaky paint and, often, a reserved band in the handle zone. The graffiti cannot be dated by their context, since no meaningful stratification could be observed at the site. But the researches of R. S. Young have shown that such vessels were made during the late 8th and 7th centuries B.C. and not before.[6] The Hymettos graffiti can thus be dated to these periods.

Prior to Young's studies much of the pottery of these periods was imperfectly understood and was dated much earlier in the Geometric period. When Blegen excavated on Hymettos and found fragments of plain one-handled cups with incised inscriptions, he assigned them to the middle of the 8th century, basing his dating on what was known, and thought, about Geometric pottery at the time. A few years later, Rhys Carpenter cast doubt on the dating of the inscribed Hymettos cups.[7] He believed that they belonged to the " Geometric Overlap ", a time in the early 7th century when degenerate Geometric pottery was still being made. Young provided the archaeological proof of Carpenter's suggestion by showing that the Hymettos cups were based on Geometric types, but that they themselves were Sub-geometric, i. e. survivals of Geometric forms which lasted a surprisingly long time into the 7th century.[8] Further evidence from the Athenian Agora and the Kerameikos has shown that Young's dating of this cup type is beyond doubt.[9]

---

[5] C. W. Blegen, *A.J.A.* 38, 1934, pp. 10-28; R. S. Young, *A.J.A.* 44, 1940, pp. 1-9. The graffiti published by Blegen are in the National Museum, Athens. Those published by Young and the unpublished pieces are in the Agora Museum, Stoa of Attalos. There are an additional 380 uninventoried sherds each preserving traces of inscribed strokes although too little to determine the letters represented. I was unable to make any joins between these sherds and the inventoried pieces.

[6] *Hesperia* 7, 1938, pp. 412-415; *A.J.A.* 46, 1942, pp. 46-47.

[7] *A.J.A.* 42, 1938, pp. 61-62.

[8] For correction of Blegen's dating of Hymettos graffiti, see Young, *Hesperia,* Suppl. II, 1939, p. 227, note 5.

[9] For the Agora evidence, see Brann, *Hesperia* 30, 1961, pp. 337-338, F 38; for material from the Kerameikos, *Kerameikos* VI, 2, pp. 168-170.

CATALOGUE

The inscriptions are arranged in groups according to their content. For the most part they are standard sanctuary dedications. A number of them express customary formulas such as " So-and-so dedicated me to Zeus." These are presented first. Next come the graffiti which are non-dedicatory, but consist of fragmentary abecedaria or simple sentences such as " So-and-so wrote me." The catalogue concludes with the fragments preserving parts of names and words, and with the great majority: the miscellaneous lot of sherds with only a few letters preserved.

All of the inventoried Hymettos graffiti, including those previously published, are catalogued here. A photograph and a drawing, both at 1:1, generally accompany each inscription, with the exception of those published by Blegen, which are well illustrated elsewhere.[10]

To avoid repetition not every fragment will receive a detailed description. Unless stated otherwise all pieces may be assumed to belong to Phaleron cups or Subgeometric skyphoi similar to the types described above, which range in date through most of the 7th century B.C. Although complete examples can usually be dated to a particular quarter within that century, in most cases a closer dating than " seventh century " is not possible for the Hymettos sherds because of their fragmentary nature. A date will be given only in the case of more complete vessels and sherds from other shapes and periods.

The fabric in most cases is Attic, pinkish to brownish buff in color, with some grit and flakes of mica. The paint is black or brown, of poor quality, and carelessly and unevenly applied.

Most of the inscriptions were incised on the outside of the vessel with a sharp point after firing.[11] The writing is usually upright in relation to the top of the vase; only differences will be noted.

The exact provenience of each graffito sherd is not recorded since it is stratigraphically unimportant. " Votive dump " means that the piece was found in the depression with the large, unstratified mass of pottery, and "Altar area " that it came from around the foundation just above the depression, to the west. A few inscriptions found at the foundation northwest of the depression are labeled " Heroon ".

---

[10] Besides Blegen's original publication in *A.J.A.* 38, 1934, the drawings, but not the photographs, are reproduced in a German translation of Blegen's article in *Das Alphabet,* ed. Gerhard Pfohl, Darmstadt, 1968, pp. 117-142.

[11] Often the surface of a sherd was too worn to determine when the inscription was incised, but there is no certain example of an inscription incised before firing.

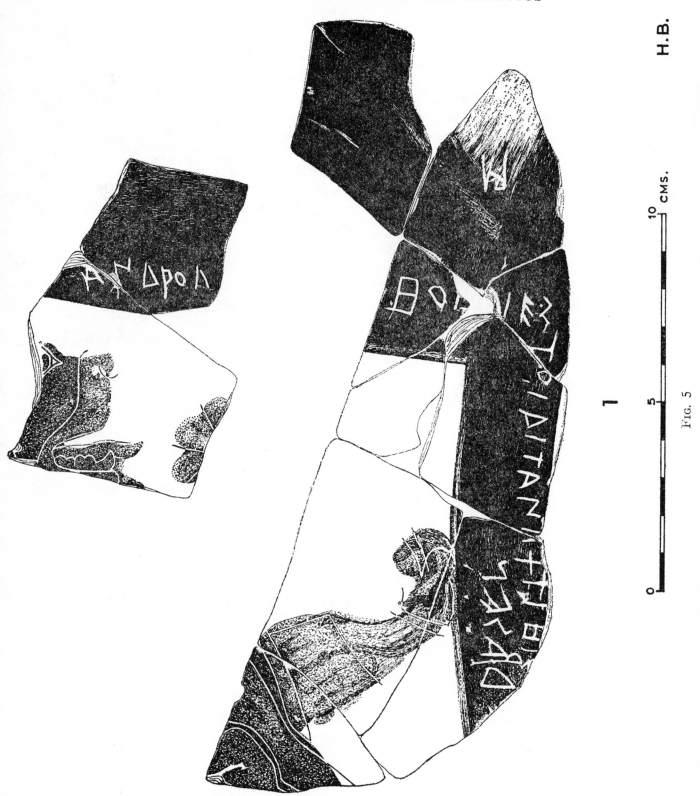

FIG. 5

DEITY AND ANEΘEKEN INSCRIPTIONS

1. Fragmentary amphora or olpe.

Fig. 5; Pl. 2.

H 163. Votive dump. *A.J.A.* 44, 1940, p. 6, no. 2.

Eleven pieces comprising two non-joining fragments. To Young's publication of six pieces are now added five more, two of which help to complete the inscription.

Part of the side wall with reserved panel preserved; panel filled with lion walking right. Cursory incision used for interior details of lion, and added red for tongue and snout; large incised rosette in front of lion. The lion is of the very early black-figure style: cf. *Kerameikos* VI, 2, pp. 272, 326.

Fine, soft, brownish buff clay, slightly micaceous; dull, somewhat worn black to bluish black glaze, outside only; thin, streaky brown to black glaze for lion and rosette.

Inscription along two sides of panel in three lines: line 1, left to right, sideways to vase, running from top to bottom, no letters missing at ends; line 2, left to right, upside down to vase, several letters missing at right; line 3, retrograde, upside down to vase, several letters possibly missing at right. Letters incised deeply but not too carefully with a blunt point.

> Line 1: Ἀνδρογ[－－－] ho Δ[..]ιϵϛ
> Line 2: τôι Δὶ τ' ἄναχτι hισ-
> Line 3: ἔδρασϵν

Line 1 contains a proper name, Androg...., followed by a patronymic or an ethnic. The final sigma is reversed, as is not uncommon in early inscriptions.

In line 2 Δί for the dative of Ζεύς is a misspelling or unusual spelling for Attica, where Διί is expected. Also strange is ἄναχτι instead of ἄνακτι although this is perhaps an early example of the Attic tendency to aspirate stops: cf. C. D. Buck, *The Greek Dialects*, Chicago, 1955, pp. 60-61.

On the rarity of Anax as a title of Zeus, see B. Hemberg, ΑΝΑΞ, ΑΝΑΣΣΑ *und* ΑΝΑΚΕΣ, Uppsala, 1955, pp. 8, 11. But the tau after Δί

may represent an elision of τϵ instead of τôι in which case the title may belong to another deity mentioned in the missing part of line 2. Hemberg shows that Apollo receives the title Anax in Homer and Classical literature far more often than any other deity, and since, like Zeus, Apollo was worshipped on Mount Hymettos (Pausanias, I, 32, 2), it is possible that the inscription is a dedication to both deities.

Line 2 breaks off with hισ[－－－] which suggests a form of ἵστημι, although the present tense would be odd.

Line 3 continues boustrophedon from line 2 and preserves only one word, ἔδρασϵν. The ends of the three horizontals of the initial epsilon are preserved at the right edge. Young would take the verb to be equivalent to ἔγραφσϵν and translate the whole, "Androg ..., son of D ..., made (i. e. wrote) ... (a dedication) ... to Zeus Anax." In other words the dedicator is stressing his proud feat, that he actually wrote a sentence. But the usage of δράω for γράφω would be unparalleled. Nor, I think, should the verb be equated with ποιέω and Androg .... or someone mentioned in the lacuna be considered the maker of the vase. As M. H. Jameson points out to me, δράω should have more force, referring possibly to the performance of a rite, as it does in *I.G.*, I², 4. The length of the lacuna at the end of line 2 and beginning of line 3 cannot be determined but it seems clear that we are dealing with a more complex text than one involving the simple fact of writing.

To the right of the end of line 1 is a lone four-barred sigma, larger and more deeply cut than the letters of the inscription. The sigma faces right, but no letters can be seen to its right because the surface there is badly worn.

Ca. 600 B.C.

2. Base fragment of a closed vessel.

Fig. 6; Pl. 2.

H 232. Votive dump.

Fragment from the lower wall and bottom of a closed vessel with flat bottom.

Inscription incised on the inside of the sherd

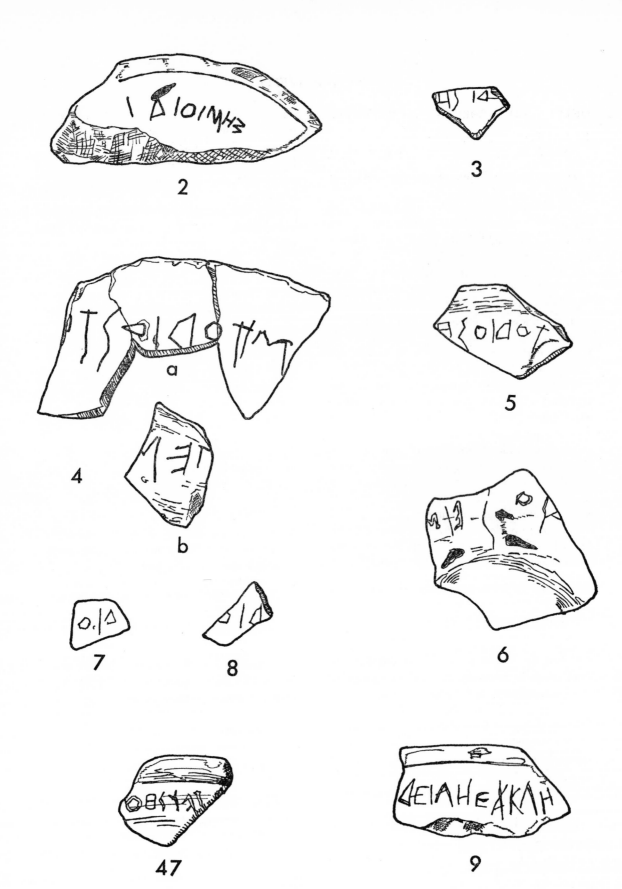

Fig. 6

after the pot was broken. It is complete and written retrograde.

$$\Sigma\eta\mu\hat{o}\iota\ \Delta\acute{\iota}$$

This epithet is not attested elsewhere, but it must express the idea of Sign-giving Zeus from σημεῖον or σῆμα, a sign of the gods. That a weather sign is meant is suggested by the fact that the term διοσημία was used later, especially at Athens to denote atmospheric phenomena: cf. Cook, *Zeus* II, pp. 4-5. For Zeus the Sign-giver (Zeus Semaleos) on Mount Parnes, see Appendix B.

Seventh century B.C.

3. Body fragment.   Fig. 6; Pl. 2.

H 213. Votive dump.
Retrograde.

$$-\Delta I\Sigma H-$$

This inscription may also be a dedication to Zeus Semios: Δὶ Ση[μῖοι].

4. Rim and upper-body fragments.
                                  Fig. 6; Pl. 2.

a. H 171/173. Votive dump.
Three joining pieces.
Retrograde.

$$[--\epsilon\grave{\iota}]\mu\grave{\iota}\ \tau\hat{o}\ \Delta\iota\grave{o}s\ \tau\hat{o}--$$

b. H 388. Votive dump.
Very probably from the same vessel as a.
Retrograde.

$$-\text{ΠEN}-$$

5. Rim fragment.   Fig. 6; Pl. 3.

H 216. Votive dump.
Retrograde.

$$-\tau\hat{o}\ \Delta\iota\grave{o}s\ h-$$

6. Base and lower-body fragment.
                                  Fig. 6; Pl. 3.

H 499. Heroon.
Clay not well cleaned; surface pitted.
Retrograde.

$$[--\tau\hat{o}]\ \Delta\iota\grave{o}s\ \epsilon\grave{\iota}\mu[\acute{\iota}--]$$

The first iota gives the appearance of being broken, but this is only because it crosses an unevenness of the surface.

7. Rim fragment.   Fig. 6; Pl. 3.

H 522. Altar area.
Grayish clay, probably burned.
Letters incised retrograde on inside of rim.

$$-\Delta\iota\acute{o}[s--]$$

8. Body fragment.   Fig. 6; Pl. 3.

H 383. Votive dump.
Retrograde.

$$-\Delta\iota\acute{o}[s--]$$

9. Rim fragment.   Fig. 6; Pl. 3.

H 130. Heroon. *A.J.A.* 44, 1940, p. 6, no. 4.
Left to right.

$$-\delta\epsilon\iota a\ h\epsilon\langle\rho\rangle a\kappa\lambda\eta[\acute{\epsilon}\epsilon\iota--]$$

Young's suggestion that the hero Herakles is mentioned is still the best solution, since the preserved letters point to that name. But with −δεια indicating a female dedicator the reading hε 'Ακλη− as a patronymic might be possible.

10. Fragment of an oinochoe.

H 71 (NM 16115). Votive dump. *A.J.A.* 38, 1934, p. 20, no. 15.
Left to right.

$$\Gamma\acute{a}\epsilon s$$

If this is a genitive of Gaia, as Blegen suggested, it is surprising. Ge and its forms are normal in Attic epigraphy, while Gaia is poetic. But unless the letters are counted as nonsense, I can come up with no better solution. For more on the Earth goddess, see Appendix A.

11. Body fragment.   Fig. 7; Pl. 3.

H 217. Votive dump.
Mended from two pieces.
Retrograde.

$$[--\grave{a}\nu]\acute{\epsilon}\theta\epsilon\kappa\epsilon-$$

12. Base and lower-body fragment.   Fig. 7.

H 162. Votive dump. *A.J.A.* 44, 1940, p. 8, no. 6.
Retrograde.

$$-\grave{a}\nu\acute{\epsilon}\theta[\epsilon\kappa\epsilon--]$$

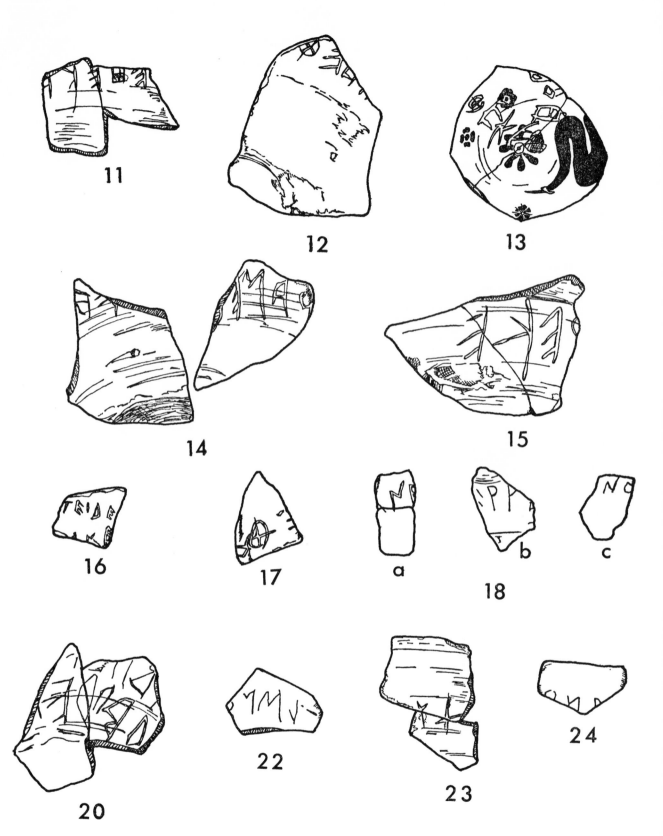

FIG. 7

13. Base fragment of a Corinthian alabastron.
Fig. 7.

H 187. Votive dump. *A.J.A.* 44, 1940, p. 6, no. 1.
Greenish buff Corinthian clay.
Left to right.

$$[--ἀνέ]θεκε\ ho.-$$

We might have expected ἀνέθεκεν in this and the following two inscriptions. The great majority of early Attic dedicatory inscriptions use the movable nu here, the only exceptions being where space or meter demand the shorter form: cf. A. E. Raubitschek, *Dedications from the Athenian Acropolis,* Cambridge, Mass., 1949, pp. 446-447. The erratic use of movable nu among the Hymettos inscriptions (**1** and **27** do use it) is simply an indication that we are dealing with a period before any customary usage was recognized and practiced.
Early Corinthian.

14. Fragments from the base and lower body.
Fig. 7; Pl. 3.

H 146 a, b. Altar area. *A.J.A.* 44, 1940, p. 8, no. 8.
Two non-joining sherds from the same cup. Young had only the larger fragment.
Retrograde.

$$-.ἀνέθ[εκ]ε\ h[ο--]$$

15. Upper-body and rim fragment.
Fig. 7; Pl. 3.

H 408. Votive dump.
Mended from two pieces.
Retrograde.

$$[--ἀνέ]θεκε$$

16. Body fragment. Fig. 7; Pl. 3.

H 175. Votive dump.
Left to right in two lines.

Line 1: −ΤΕΙΔΕ−
Line 2: −ἀνέ[θεκε−−]

17. Body fragment. Fig. 7; Pl. 3.

H 516. Altar area.
Retrograde.

$$[--ἀν]έθε[κε--]$$

18. Body fragments. Fig. 7; Pl. 3.

a. H 532. Altar area.
Mended from two pieces.
Left to right.

$$- ἀνέ[θεκε--]$$

b. H 531. Altar area.
A non-joining fragment from the same vessel as a.
Left to right.

$$- ΕΡΥ -$$

c. H 533. Altar area.
Probably from the same vessel as a and b.
Left to right.

$$- ΝΟ -$$

19. Body fragments.

H 73 (NM 16125), H 74 (NM 16132), H 75 (NM 16128). Votive dump. *A.J.A.* 38, 1934, p. 20, nos. 16-18.
Three non-joining fragments of the same vessel.

$$-ΠΕΡΙ[------- ἀνέ]θεν$$

See also **29.**

ABECEDARIA AND ΕΓΡΑΦΣΕ
INSCRIPTIONS

20. Fragment from the base and lower body.
Fig. 7; Pl. 4.

H 165/184. Votive dump. *A.J.A.* 44, 1940, p. 8, no. 9.
Two joining sherds.
Two lines retrograde.

Line 1: − ΑΒΓΔΕ −
Line 2: − ΑΒΓΔΕF −

Two incomplete abecedaria, perhaps of teacher and pupil. In the second line the delta resembles a Boiotian or Euboian type, but this is probably only the result of a slip of the stylus in the hand of an inexperienced writer. The other letters in this line are also misshapen and should probably be explained likewise.

The sixth letter of the second line preserves only the lower part of a vertical stroke. This cannot be zeta, but must be part of a digamma. The presence of digamma in the Attic abecedarium agrees well with Jeffery's argument that an illiterate people, in acquiring literacy, would receive wholesale the alphabet of its teacher (*L.S.A.G.*, pp. 1-4). In so doing, the illiterates would encounter certain superfluous letters which had no sound value in their dialect, and which they would never or rarely use in writing. They would retain such letters in their abecedarium, however, since they lacked the critical judgment and experience to emend the new alphabet to their own needs. Digamma had no phonetic value in the Attic alphabet (attested only in two poetic metrical inscriptions: Jeffery, *L.S.A.G.*, p. 76, no. 7, a dedication of the 7th century B.C.; p. 77, no. 23, a 6th century grave monument), but its presence is explained by Jeffery's discussion. Mabel Lang has published several 7th and 6th century abecedaria from the Athenian Agora which also contain digamma (*The Athenian Agora*, XXI, *Graffiti and Dipinti*, Princeton, 1976). It should be noted that digamma kept its place in the developed Attic alphabet because it was used in the alphabetic numeral system of Attica: cf. M. N. Tod, *B.S.A.* 45, 1950, p. 135.

21. Shallow plate.

H 2 (NM 16114). Votive dump. *A.J.A.* 38, 1934, p. 15, no. 10; Jeffery, *L.S.A.G.*, p. 69, pl. 1, no. *3c*.

The inscription is complete, written left to right.

ΑΒΓ

Seventh century B.C.

22. Body fragment.   Fig. 7; Pl. 4.
H 501. Altar area.
Retrograde.

– . ΛΜΝΟ –

It is interesting to note that here, and prob-

ably in **24**, the writer omitted Ionic xi from his abecedarium. He did not include it automatically as did the inscriber of **20** the digamma.

23. Fragment from the rim and upper body.
                                Fig. 7; Pl. 4.
H 170. Votive dump.
Mended from two pieces.
Left to right.

– ΥΧ –

24. Body fragment.   Fig. 7; Pl. 4.
H 238. Votive dump.
Retrograde.

– ΜΝΟ –

25. Body fragment.   Fig. 8; Pl. 4.
H 539. Altar area.
Grayish buff clay.
Left to right.

– ΒΓΔΕ –

26. Fragmentary one-handled cup.

H 69 (NM 16121), H 70 (NM 16116). Votive dump. *A.J.A.* 38, 1934, p. 18, nos. 13-14.
Two non-joining fragments of the same cup. Left to right.

ΛΜ[– – – – – –]ΠΡ   Χ

27. Fragmentary cup.   Fig. 8; Pl. 4.
H 189. Votive dump. *A.J.A.* 44, 1940, p. 8, no. 11.
Mended from three pieces.
Retrograde.

– . ℎόσπερ ἔγραφσεν –

The inscriber forgot to write both the final rho of ὅσπερ and the verb's augment. He later realized his mistake and added the missing letters. He squeezed the rho into its proper place by making it tall and narrow, but this left no room for the augment of the verb, so he put

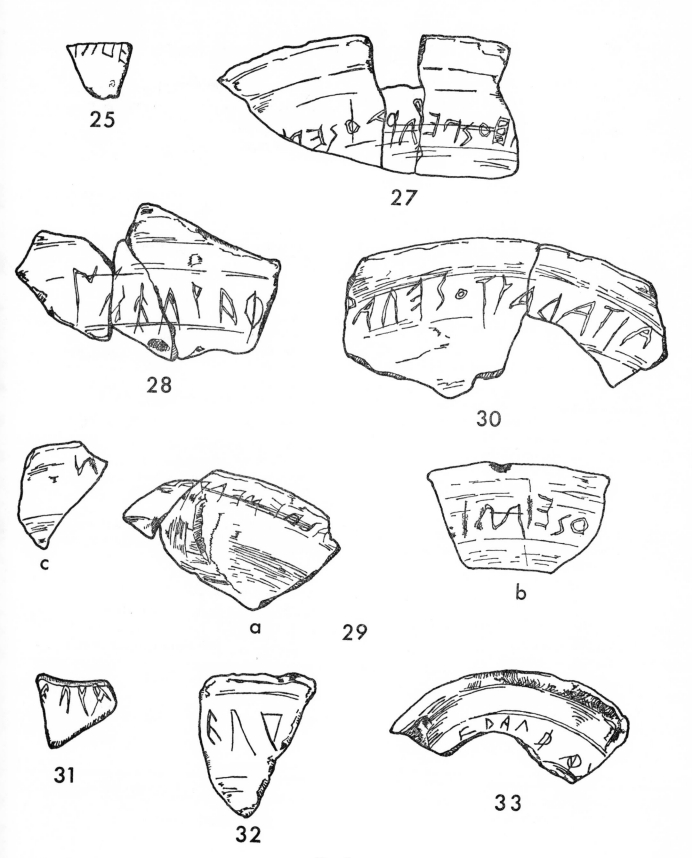

Fig. 8

it just below and slightly to the right of the rho. Both added letters come right on a break and are partly obliterated.

28. Rim fragment. Fig. 8; Pl. 4.

H 147. Altar area. *A.J.A.* 44, 1940, p. 8, no. 7.
Mended from three pieces.
Left to right.

$$\text{ΝΙΣ } ἔγραφ[σε--]$$

29. Fragments of a skyphos. Fig. 8; Pl. 4.

a. H 223. Votive dump. *A.J.A.* 44, 1940, p. 8, no. 5.
Two joining pieces of a small, shoulderless skyphos with reserved handle zone.
Retrograde.

$$-ας δὲ μ' ἔγραφ[σε--]$$

b. H 215. Votive dump. *A.J.A.* 44, 1940, p. 6, no. 3.
Very likely from the same skyphos as a.
Retrograde.

$$-ος εἰμί-$$

c. H 181. Votive dump.
Probably from the same vessel as a and b. The sherd preserves a single letter, nu, written retrograde. It is apparently the final letter of the inscription, since no letters follow to the left.
Taking the three fragments together we may restore the inscription to read something like

$$[τô Δι]ὸς εἰμί. [---]ας δὲ μ' ἔγραφ[σε]ν.$$

30. One-handled cup fragment. Fig. 8; Pl. 4.

H 156. Votive dump. *A.J.A.* 44, 1940, p. 8, no. 10.
Mended from two pieces.
Retrograde.

$$-αι τάδ' αὐτὸς ἐγ⟨ρ⟩αφ[σε--]$$

31. Body fragment. Fig. 8; Pl. 5.

H 387. Votive dump.
Grayish buff clay.
Left to right.

$$-ἔγρα[φσε--]$$

32. Rim fragment. Fig. 8; Pl. 5.

H 135. Heroon.
Left to right.

$$-ἔγρ[αφσε--]$$

33. Fragment from the floor and ring foot of a black-glazed kylix. Fig. 8; Pl. 5.

H 402. Votive dump.
Letters incised left to right on underside of foot.

$$-ΕΡΑΓΦΑ-$$

The inscriber apparently tried to write the word ἔγραφσε but made several mistakes which he tried to correct. The final preserved letter is an alpha written over an omicron, and preceding that some letter seems to have been changed into a phi.
Sixth century B.C.

34. Body fragments. Fig. 9; Pl. 5.

a. H 545. Altar area.
Two lines retrograde. The upper line preserves only traces; in the lower line

$$[--ἔγ]ραφ[σε---]$$

b-f. Similarities in fabric, glaze, and letter forms suggest that these small fragments, all from the votive dump, belong to the same vessel as **34** a.

b. H 546. Retrograde. $-.Α-$
c. H 547. Left to right? $-ΥΣΙΠ.-$
d. H 548. Left to right? $-.ΛΟ-$
    (Photograph upside down.)
e. H 549. Retrograde. $-.Ν.-$
f. H 551. Either way. $-ΙΤ.-$

The inscription is apparently in two lines, boustrophedon.

35. Rim fragment. Fig. 9; Pl. 5.

H 537. Altar area.
Grayish clay.
Left to right.

$$-ἔγρα[φσε--]$$

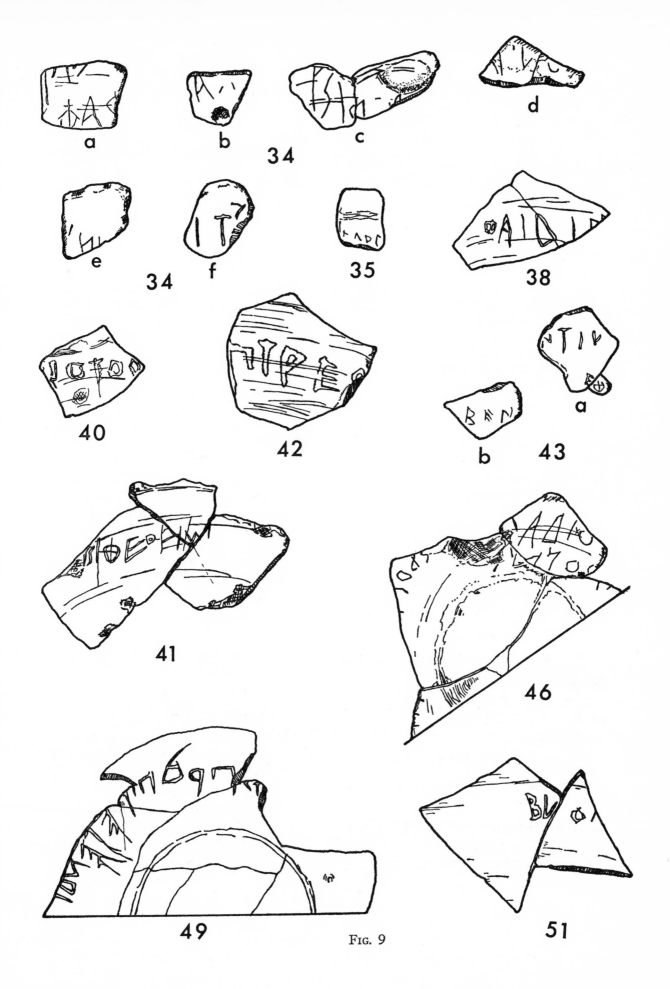

FIG. 9

The readings are those of Young before the sherd was washed. Most of the letter traces disappeared in washing.

NAMES AND OTHER WORDS

36. One-handled cup.

H 1 (NM 16092). Votive dump. *A.J.A.* 38, 1934, p. 10, no. 1; Jeffery, *L.S.A.G.*, p. 69, pl. 1, no. 3*b*.

The inscription spirals retrograde around the vase. Jeffery proposes the following (*L.S. A.G.*, p. 401): Νι[ϙό]δεμος (Μ[ενέ]δεμος?) Φ[ιλ]αμίδες καταπύγον. Λεό[φρα]δες [ερι].

For a study of vituperative graffiti with the word καταπύγων, see M. Milne and D. von Bothmer, *Hesperia* 22, 1953, pp. 215-224.

Third quarter of the seventh century B.C.

37. Rim fragment.

H 54 (NM 16117). Votive dump. *A.J.A.* 38, 1934, p. 12, no. 3; J. Kirchner, *Imagines Inscriptionum Atticarum,* 2nd ed., Berlin, 1948, p. 9, no. 3.

Two lines retrograde.

Line 1: – Τλεσίας –
Line 2: –.Α.–

38. Body fragment.   Fig. 9; Pl. 5.

H 174. Votive dump.
Mended from two pieces.
Incised with a blunt point left to right.

– ΦΑΙΔΙΜ –

The name Φαίδιμ[ος –] is a likely restoration.

39. Rim fragment.

H 68 (NM 16119). Votive dump. *A.J.A.* 38, 1934, p. 15, no. 8.
Retrograde.

– ΑΥΤΟΜΕ –

Blegen suggested a personal name such as Αὐτομέ[δον – –].

40. Body fragment.   Fig. 9; Pl. 5.

H 234. Votive dump.
Letters incised left to right with a dull point.

– ΔΟΤΟΣ –

A personal name such as [– ἱερό]δοτος is possible.

41. Body fragment.   Fig. 9; Pl. 5.

H 177. Votive dump.
Mended from three pieces.
Left to right.

– ΙΣΙΘΕΟ εἰμί

The first six letters are probably the end of a personal name in the genitive, perhaps [Δε]ισιθέο. The inscription is a statement of ownership: " I am (the cup) of [De]isitheos."

42. Fragment from the upper body.   Fig. 9; Pl. 5.

H 169. Votive dump.
Grayish to brown clay.
Letters shallowly incised with a blunt point, left to right.

– ΠΤΡΕΟ –

The demotic [Λαμ]πτρέο[ς] is suggested by the preserved letters, although this would seem unlikely before the time of Kleisthenes. But if the deme Lamptrai did not exist at the time of this dedication, the district or town surely did. If not a toponymic, the letters are probably part of a personal name.

43. Body fragments.   Fig. 9; Pl. 6.

a. H 154. Altar area.
   Once mended from two pieces, the smaller now missing.
   Two lines left to right.

Line 1: – ΝΤΙΛ –
Line 2: ΕΘ –

The letters in the first line suggest the name ['Α]ντίλ[οχος]. For the second line we may restore ἔθ[εκε – –].

b. H 155. Altar area.
   Mended from two pieces; from the same vessel as a.
   Left to right.

– ΒΕΝ –

44. Rim fragment.

H 61 (NM 16126). Votive dump. *A.J.A.*
38, 1934, p. 24, no. 22.
Good black glaze.
Retrograde, the writing upside down to
vessel.

– OPOΘ –

Blegen suggested the personal name
[Δ]oρoθ[έos].
Sixth century B.C.

45. Rim fragment.

H 64 (NM 16129). Votive dump. *A.J.A.*
38, 1934, p. 13, no. 6.
Retrograde.

EYΘ –

The letters may be the beginning of a personal name.

46. Base and lower-body fragment.
                                    Fig. 9; Pl. 6.
H 542. Altar area.
Four joining sherds; brownish to grayish
buff clay.
Two lines retrograde.

Line 1: – OIΔA (traces)
Line 2: (traces) ONEYΣ

Line 2 ends with a personal name or ethnic.

47. ʹRim fragment.   Fig. 6; Pl. 6.
H 167. Votive dump.
Retrograde.

– τevs ho –

48. Rim fragment.   Fig. 11, Pl. 6.
H 148. Altar area.
Left to right.

– hOEΦ .–

Part of a personal name such as
ho Ἐφ[ίππου].

49. Fragmentary cup or skyphos. Fig. 9; Pl. 6.

H 190. Votive dump. *A.J.A.* 44, 1940, p. 8,
no. 12.
Mended from four pieces.
Letters incised retrograde with a blunt point
which often slipped, leaving long, shallow
scratches.

–.s πρόπιϝε τενδί

Young believed the inscription to be a dedication to Zeus, the final two letters mentioning the
deity in the dative case. But without the definite article this would be very unusual. Miss
Jeffery has suggested to me that the reading
should be τενδί = τηνδί with -δι as the epideictic
iota which is often found in vase inscriptions.
The graffito says " Drink *this* up."

50. One-handled cup.

H 6 (NM 16091). Votive dump. *A.J.A.* 38,
1934, p. 12, no. 2; Jeffery, *L.S.A.G.*, p. 69,
pl. 1, no. 3a.
Inscribed retrograde in two lines.

Line 1: –.EMAΔPO...I...TAΦIΛEITE–
Line 2: –..ATAX.....E.APA

For the first line Jeffery suggests (*L.S.A.G.*,
p. 401) [––]εμ' ἀ⟨ν⟩δρὸ[s ?μ]ά[λισ]τα φιλεῖ
τε[––], while for the end of the line P. Kret-
schmer, *Glotta* 26, 1938, p. 35 proposes *name*
φιλεῖ τ[ὸν ––] (or τ[ἐν ––]).
Early seventh century B.C.

51. Body fragment of a Corinthian-type
skyphos.   Fig. 9; Pl. 6.

H 227/240. Votive dump.
Light pinkish buff clay burned gray; thick,
dull black glaze. Mended from two pieces.
Left to right.

BΛOι –

If the final stroke is taken as part of a sigma,
we may restore the word βλοσ[υρός], " virile ",
or " grim."
Ca. 625-600 B.C.

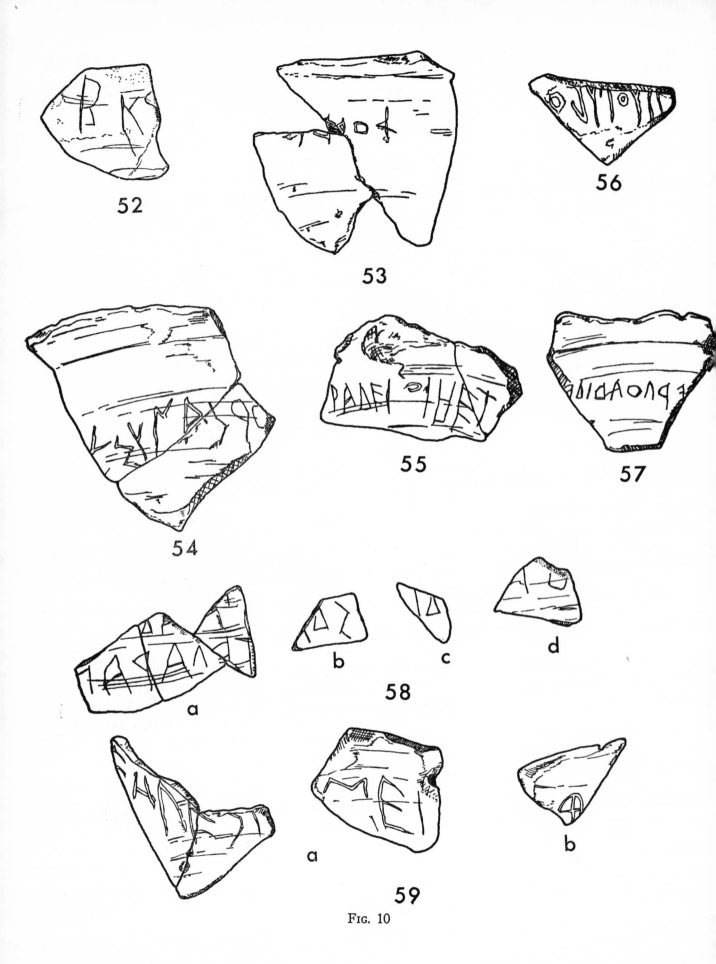

Fig. 10

52. Body fragment. Fig. 10; Pl. 6.

H 182. Votive dump.

Letters incised left to right, upside down to vessel.

ΒΛΟ–

The second letter is a lambda. What looks like a diagonal stroke at the upper right of the letter is only a scratch. The inscription may read βλο[συρός – –].

53. Body fragment. Fig. 10; Pl. 6.

H 179. Votive dump.
Mended from two pieces.
Retrograde.

ΧΟΡΔ.–

We could restore χορδ[έ], " gut ", or " string of a lyre ", or one of several words involving the strings of a musical instrument formed on the stem χορδ–.

54. Fragment from the rim and body.
Fig. 10; Pl. 7.

H 534. Votive dump.
Mended from two pieces.
Left to right.

ΧΣΥΝΑΣϘΟ–

The letters suggest to me ξυνασκέω, " train ", or " exercise ".

55. Body fragment. Fig. 10; Pl. 6.

H 131. Heroon.
Grayish buff clay; mended from two pieces.
Left to right.

–ΡΑΔΕΙΟΙΗΕΤΑ–

Miss Jeffery suggested to me [– – θεοφ]ράδει οἱ hετα[ῖροι – –]. Note the psilosis of hοι before heta.

56. Upper-body fragment. Fig. 10; Pl. 6.

H 237. Votive dump.
Retrograde.

–ΔΥΟΠΥΛΟ–

Perhaps – δύο πυλô[ν – –] or part of a personal name.

MISCELLANEOUS INSCRIPTIONS

57. Fragment from the rim and upper body.
Fig. 10; Pl. 7.

H 219. Votive dump.
Retrograde.

–ΕΡΓΟΑΔΙΔΕ–

58. Body fragments. Fig. 10; Pl. 7.

a. H 521. Altar area.
Mended from three pieces.
Two lines retrograde.

Line 1: (traces) ΑΔ–
Line 2: –ΤΕΓΑΡΑΠ–

b-d. Three small fragments probably from the same vessel as a. Votive dump.

b. H 525. Either way. –.ΔΣ–
c. H 526. Either way. –ΙΔ–
d. H 535. Either way. –ΙΟ–

59. Fragments of a closed vessel.
Fig. 10; Pl. 7.

a. H 518 a, b. Votive dump.
Two non-joining fragments, one mended from two pieces.
Left to right.

a) –ΕΑΓΕΣΙ–
b) –ΜΕΙ–

b. H 212. Votive dump.
A small fragment from the same vessel as a, preserving a single letter, theta.
Seventh century B.C.?

60. Body fragment. Fig. 11; Pl. 7.

H 389/406. Votive dump.
Mended from three pieces.
Left to right in two lines.

Line 1: –ΛΟΤΕ.–
Line 2: –ΟΗΑΟ.–

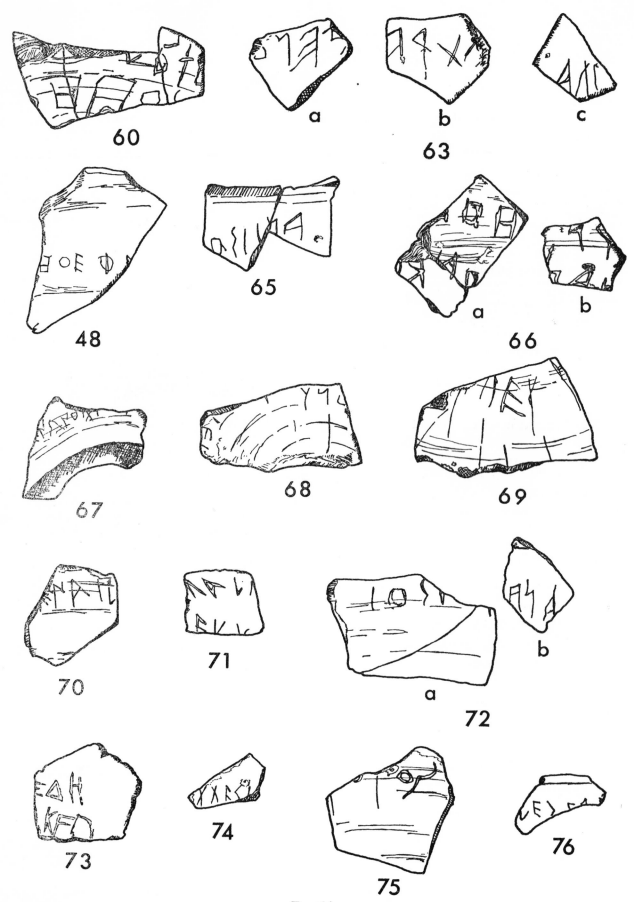

FIG. 11

61. Body fragment.

H 67 (NM 16130). Votive dump. *A.J.A.* 38, 1934, p. 15, no. 7.
Retrograde.

–ΤΑΥΤΕ.–

62. Rim fragment.

H 62 (NM 16123). Votive dump. *A.J.A.* 38, 1934, p. 13, no. 4; J. Kirchner, *Imagines Inscriptionum Atticarum*, 2nd ed., Berlin, 1948, p. 9, no. 2.
Retrograde.

–ΟΤΕΠΙΝ–

63. Body fragments.   Fig. 11; Pl. 8.

Three non-joining fragments very likely from the same vessel. Altar area.

a. H 199. Retrograde. –ΜΕΝΟ–
b. H 198. Retrograde. –.ΧΡΕ–
c. H 197. Retrograde? –ΙΓΑ–

64. Upper-body fragment.

H 66 (NM 16124). Votive dump. *A.J.A.* 38, 1934, p. 18, no. 12.
Left to right.

– ΘΟΝΜ–

65. Upper-body fragment.   Fig. 11; Pl. 7.

H 506. Altar area.
Mended from two pieces.
Letters incised retrograde with a blunt point.

ΑΝΙΙΣΟ–

66. Body fragments.   Fig. 11; Pl. 8.

Two non-joining fragments very likely from the same vessel. Heroon.

a. H 136/142.
   Two lines, the lower retrograde, the upper probably so.

   Line 1: – ΗΟ. –
   Line 2: – ΠΝΚ–

b. H 141.
   Two lines, both probably retrograde.

Line 1: –ΣΑ–
Line 2: –.ΑΣ–

67. Base fragment.   Fig. 11; Pl. 7.

H 228. Votive dump.
Resting surface and lower body reserved; gray clay.
Left to right.

–ΕΝΓΝΟ.–

68. Lower-body fragment.   Fig. 11; Pl. 8.

H 180. Votive dump.
Retrograde.

–ΟΝΥ......Ε.–

69. Body fragment.   Fig. 11; Pl. 8.

H 145. Altar area.
Grayish buff clay.
Two lines, the upper left to right, the lower probably the same; both lines upside down to vessel. The lower line preserves only traces; in the upper line

–..ΕΥ.–

70. Upper-body fragment.   Fig. 11; Pl. 8.

H 220. Votive dump.
Left to right.

–ΕΝΑΙΛ–

71. Upper-body fragment.   Fig. 11; Pl. 8.

H 176. Votive dump.
Two lines left to right.

   Line 1: –ΓΑΛΙ–
   Line 2: –ΕΚΚ–

72. Body fragments.   Fig. 11; Pl. 8.

Two non-joining fragments, probably from the same vessel. Votive dump.

a. H 161. Retrograde. – .ΣΟΙ
b. H 195. Retrograde. –ΑΝΑ–

73. Body fragment of a cooking-ware vessel.
          Fig. 11; Pl. 8.

H 137. Heroon.

Micaceous brown clay, unglazed; surface much pitted; handmade.

Letters shallowly incised in two lines left to right.

> Line 1: –EΔH
> Line 2: –KE.

The second letter of line 2 is an epsilon whose lower horizontal is broken away.

74. Body fragment.   Fig. 11; Pl. 8.

H 413. Votive dump.
Left to right.

> –XΓEΣI–

75. Rim fragment.   Fig. 11; Pl. 8.

H 164. Votive dump.
Letters incised left to right with a blunt point.

> –.OΠOΣ

76. Rim fragment.   Fig. 11; Pl. 8.

H 185. Votive dump.
Grayish buff clay.
Left to right.

> – ΛEṢM.–

77. Upper-body fragment.

H 63 (NM 16120). Votive dump. *A.J.A.* 38, 1934, p. 13, no. 5.

Two lines retrograde. Traces of letters in the second line; in the first line

> –TIΣTO–

78. Body fragments.   Fig. 12; Pl. 9.

Three separate pieces probably belonging to the same vessel. Votive dump.

a. H 208. Left to right. –MAΣE–
b. H 411. Probably left to right. –TAI
c. H 211. Left to right. ΠO–

79. Lower-body fragment.   Fig. 12; Pl. 9.

H 509. Altar area.
Retrograde.

> –.ONΛE–

80. Body fragment.   Fig. 12; Pl. 9.

H 172. Votive dump.

Two lines, the upper left to right, the lower apparently retrograde. In the lower line, traces of at least two letters; in the upper line

> –AXIΘΣ–

81. Body fragment.   Fig. 12; Pl. 9.

H 242. Votive dump.

Letters incised upside down to vessel, probably retrograde.

> –TOIΣ

82. Body fragment.   Fig. 12; Pl. 9.

H 515. Altar area.
Two lines retrograde.

> Line 1: –OPE–
> Line 2: –.EṢ–

The second letter in the first line resembles a koppa but is probably a poorly shaped rho; we should expect kappa to precede epsilon.

83. Upper-body fragment.   Fig. 12; Pl. 9.

H 527. Altar area.
Left to right.

> –KAIΓ–

84. Fragment from the rim and body.
          Fig. 12; Pl. 9.

H 149. Altar area.
Mended from three pieces.
Retrograde.

> –ΛONOI–

85. Upper-body fragment.   Fig. 12; Pl. 9.

H 505. Altar area.
Left to right.

> –.ΛETE–

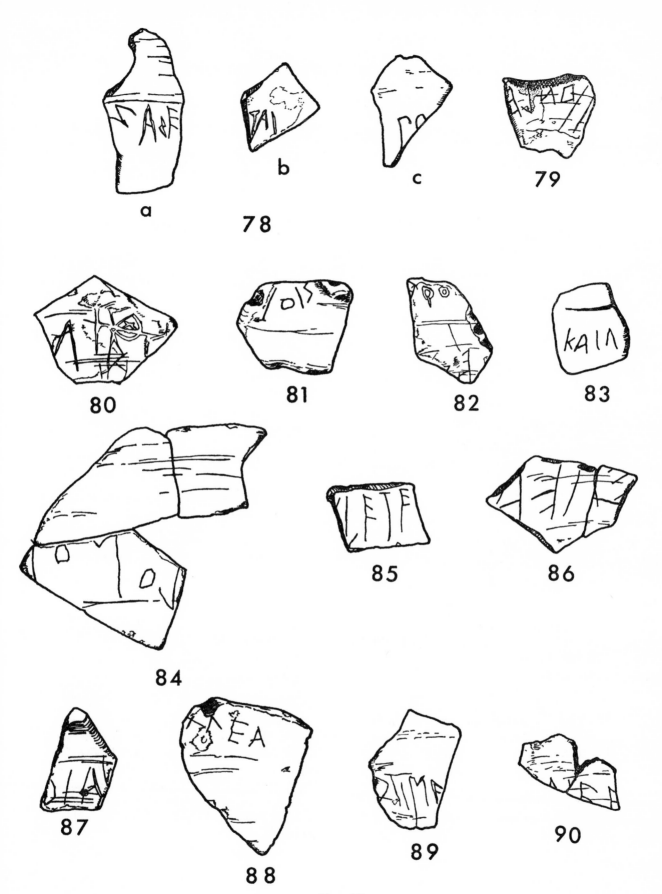

a

78

b

c

79

80

81

82

83

84

85

86

87

88

89

90

Fig. 12

86. Body fragment. Fig. 12; Pl. 9.

H 523. Altar area.
Mended from three pieces.
Retrograde.

–ΕΓΕΑ–

87. Rim and upper-body fragment.
Fig. 12; Pl. 9.

H 386. Votive dump.
Probably retrograde.

–ΙΑΙΟ–

88. Body fragment. Fig. 12; Pl. 9.

H 132. Heroon.
Left to right.

–ΧΓΕΑ–

89. Body fragment. Fig. 12; Pl. 9.

H 188. Votive dump.
Left to right.

–ΟΤΙΜΕ–

90. Body fragment. Fig. 12; Pl. 10.

H 540. Altar area.
Gray clay, probably burned; mended from
two pieces.
Left to right.

–.ΙΕΞ–

The second letter could be a sigma with the
second bar coming on the line of the break.

91. Fragment from the upper body.
Fig. 13; Pl. 10.

H 385. Votive dump.
Retrograde.

ΣΟΣ–

92. Upper-body fragment. Fig. 13; Pl. 10.
H 412. Altar area.
Retrograde.

ΣΕΙ–

93. Upper-body fragment. Fig. 13; Pl. 10.

H 503. Altar area.
Retrograde.

ΣΙΝ–

94. Body fragment of a black-glazed kylix.
Fig. 13; Pl. 10.

H 166. Votive dump.
Shiny black glaze outside, grayed and pitted
inside; brownish red to gray clay, probably
burned.
Letters incised upside down to vessel, probably left to right.

–ΣΑ

Sixth century B.C.

95. Rim fragment. Fig. 13; Pl. 10.

H 168. Votive dump.
Retrograde.

–.ΜΙ

96. Body fragment. Fig. 13; Pl. 10.

H 529. Altar area.
Retrograde.

ΤΕ–

97. Body fragment. Fig. 13; Pl. 10.

H 221. Votive dump.
Left to right.

ΙΤΕ–

98. Rim fragment. Fig. 13; Pl. 10.

H 133. Heroon.
Left to right.

–ΟΑΣ

99. Rim fragment. Fig. 13; Pl. 10

H 134. Heroon.
Left to right.

–ΑΕ

Perhaps a ligature combining alpha and
epsilon. For graffito ligatures in general, see
Karl Lehmann, *Samothrace* 2, II, *The Inscriptions on Ceramics and Minor Objects*, New
York, 1960, p. 30, note 18. Although they
occur from the Archaic period onward, graffito
ligatures are not common until the Hellenistic
period.

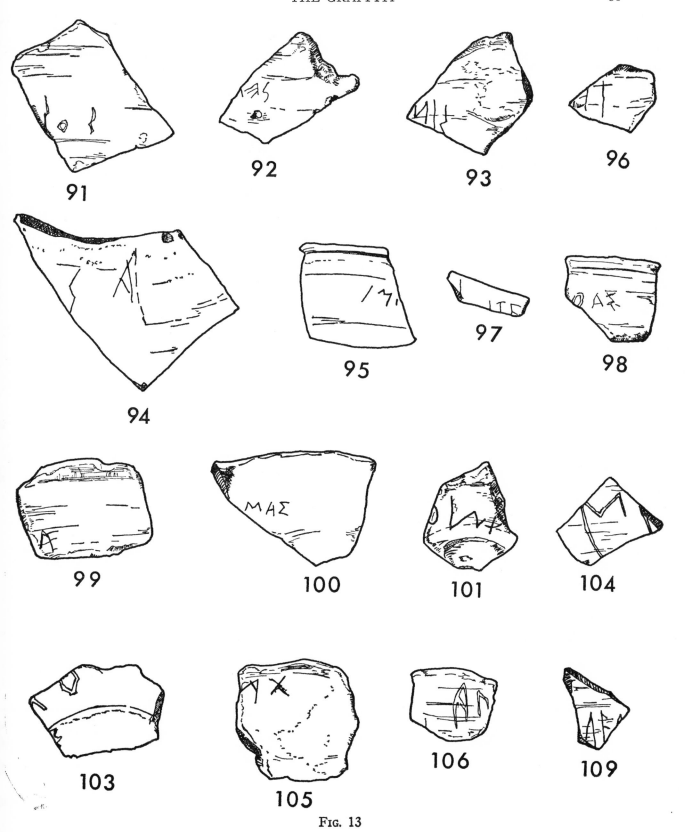

FIG. 13

100. Rim fragment.   Fig. 13; Pl. 10.

H 191. Votive dump.
Left to right.

–ΜΑΣ

101. Base fragment.   Fig. 13; Pl. 10.

H 504. Altar area.
Letters incised retrograde, upside down to
vessel, with a blunt point.

–ΟΜΕ–

102. Base fragment.

H 25 (NM 16102). Votive dump. *A.J.A.*
38, 1934, p. 16, no. 11.
Left to right.

–ΟΣ

103. Base fragment.   Fig. 13; Pl. 10.

H 409. Votive dump.
Either way.

–ΙΟ

104. Body fragment.   Fig. 13; Pl. 10.

H 511. Altar area.
Letters incised with a blunt point, left to
right.

–ΜΙ–

105. Upper-body fragment.   Fig. 13; Pl. 11.

H 508. Altar area.
Greenish buff clay with brown grit.
Retrograde.

ΧΑ–

106. Upper-body fragment.   Fig. 13; Pl. 11.

H 553. Altar area.
Gray clay, burned.
Letters incised left to right with a blunt
point.

ΑΤΤ–

107. Upper-body fragment.   Fig. 14; Pl. 11.

H 384. Votive dump.
Mended from two pieces.
Left to right.

ΡΟ–

A slip of the writing implement is responsible
for the long vertical of the rho.

108. Rim fragment.

H 72 (NM 16118). Votive dump. *A.J.A.*
38, 1934, p. 15, no. 9.
Retrograde.

ΜΥ–

109. Upper-body fragment.   Fig. 13; Pl. 11.

H 512. Altar area.
Left to right.

–ΓΕ.–

110. Rim fragment.   Fig. 14; Pl. 11.

H 241. Votive dump.
Retrograde.

–.ΔΕΕ.–

111. Body fragment.   Fig. 14; Pl. 11.

H 524. Altar area.
Left to right.

–ΕΝΟ–

112. Body fragment   Fig. 14; Pl. 11.

H 407. Votive dump.
Probably left to right.

–ΜΦΙΣ –

113. Rim fragment.   Fig. 14; Pl. 11.

H 193. Votive dump.
Retrograde.

–ΝΤΑ–

114. Upper-body fragment.   Fig. 14; Pl. 11.

H 233. Votive dump.
Left to right.

–ΗΕ–

115. Body fragment of a closed vessel.
Fig. 14; Pl. 11.

H 404. Votive dump.
Good black glaze outside, unglazed inside;
mended from two pieces.

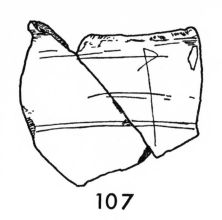

107

110

111

112

113

114

115

116

117

118

120

121

122

123

124

125

126

FIG. 14

Two lines of letters running left to right and sideways to the vessel, from top to bottom. The first line is illegible; in the second line

–ETE–

Seventh century B.C.?

116. Body fragment.   Fig. 14; Pl. 11.
H 541. Altar area.
Letters incised with a blunt point, retrograde and sideways to the vessel, from bottom to top.

–ΔAΠ–

117. Upper-body fragment.   Fig. 14; Pl. 11.
H 510. Altar area.
Letters incised with a blunt point, retrograde.

–.OYΔ–

118. Rim fragment.   Fig. 14; Pl. 11.
H 194. Votive dump.
Glaze bands outside on rim; below, apparently a dot row.
Letters incised left to right just below the rim.

–ONI–

Late Geometric II or Subgeometric.

119. Rim and body fragment of a Protoattic jug.
H 65 (NM 16113). Votive dump. *A.J.A.* 38, 1934, p. 23, no. 19.
Left to right. Complete?

AΣ

120. Rim fragment.   Fig. 14; Pl. 11.
H 405. Votive dump.
Left to right.

–ΣA–

121. Upper-body fragment.   Fig. 14; Pl. 11.
H 517. Altar area.
Left to right.

–ΠA.–

122. Body fragment.   Fig. 14; Pl. 12.
H 417. Votive dump.
Left to right.

–EI–

123. Body fragment.   Fig. 14; Pl. 12.
H 530. Altar area.
Left to right.

–MAT.–

124. Body fragment.   Fig. 14; Pl. 12.
H 200. Votive dump.
Possibly three lines; traces of letters at top and bottom; across middle, retrograde

–APX–

125. Rim fragment.   Fig. 14; Pl. 12.
H 138. Heroon.
Probably left to right.

–MI–

126. Body fragment of a Corinthian-type skyphos.   Fig. 14; Pl. 12.
H 418. Votive dump.
Good black glaze.
Letters incised retrograde with a blunt point.

–ΠA–

Late seventh or early sixth century B.C.

127. Body fragment.   Fig. 15; Pl. 12.
H 500. Heroon.
Probably left to right.

–.AIA–

128. Body fragment.   Fig. 15; Pl. 12.
H 513. Altar area.
Probably retrograde.

–ΔE–

129. Rim fragment.   Fig. 15; Pl. 12.
H 225. Votive dump.
Letters incised with a blunt point, probably retrograde.

–IA

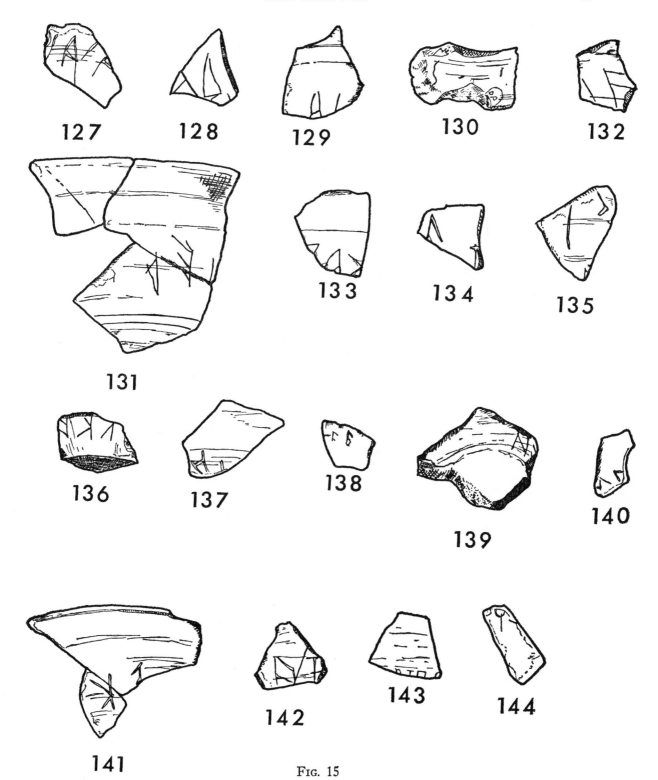

Fig. 15

130. Base fragment.   Fig. 15; Pl. 12.
H 514. Altar area.
Either way.

–Ϛ   (symbol ?)

The circular letter could be a theta, some
kind of symbol, or merely a doodle.

131. Fragment from the rim and body.
                          Fig. 15; Pl. 12.
H 231. Votive dump.
Letters incised upside down to vessel, left to
right.

–IEA.–

132. Upper-body fragment.   Fig. 15; Pl. 12.
H 536. Altar area.
Left to right.

–IE–

133. Body fragment.   Fig. 15; Pl. 12.
H 218. Votive dump.
Retrograde.

–.A.–

134. Body fragment.   Fig. 15; Pl. 12.
H 210. Votive dump.
Grayish buff clay.
Left to right.

–ET–

135. Body fragment.   Fig. 15; Pl. 12.
H 229. Votive dump.
Letters incised with a blunt point, probably
retrograde.

–ΣI–

There are traces of a second line below this.

136. Base fragment.   Fig. 15; Pl. 12.
H 224. Votive dump.
Letters incised upside down to vessel, left to
right.

–YKE–

137. Body fragment.   Fig. 15; Pl. 12.
H 209. Votive dump.
Grayish buff clay.
Letters incised with a blunt point, left to
right, apparently upside down to vessel.

–.A–

138. Body fragment.   Fig. 15; Pl. 13.
H 183. Votive dump.
Surface very worn. Left to right.

–EΓ–

139. Base fragment.   Fig. 15; Pl. 13.
H 214. Votive dump.
Retrograde.

–EN

140. Body fragment.   Fig. 15; Pl. 13.
H 415. Votive dump.
Grayish buff clay.
Letters incised with a blunt point, probably
left to right.

–ΓE–

141. Rim fragment.   Fig. 15; Pl. 13.
H 139/140. Heroon.
Two joining pieces.
Retrograde.

–EK–

142. Upper-body fragment.   Fig. 15; Pl. 13.
H 550. Altar area.
Mended from two pieces.
Left to right.

–AT–

143. Body fragment.   Fig. 15; Pl. 13.
H 230. Votive dump.
Grayish buff clay.
Probably left to right.

–.TΤ.–

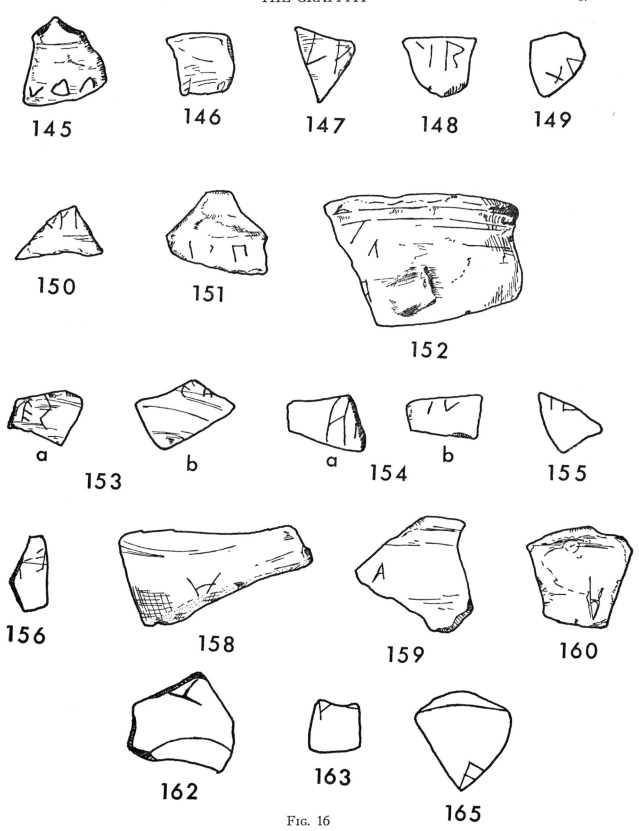

FIG. 16

144. Upper-body fragment.   Fig. 15; Pl. 13.
H 552. Altar area.
Either way.

–ΟϘ.–

145. Rim fragment.   Fig. 16; Pl. 13.
H 235. Votive dump.
Letters incised with a blunt point, probably left to right.

–ΥΔΓ–

146. Rim fragment.   Fig. 16; Pl. 13.
H 414. Votive dump.
Retrograde.

–ΠΕ–

147. Body fragment.   Fig. 16; Pl. 13.
H 192. Votive dump.
Left to right.

–ΛΥ–

148. Body fragment.   Fig. 16; Pl. 13.
H 554. Altar area.
Left to right.

–.Ρ–

The rho appears to have a tail, but this is probably the result of a slip of the writing instrument at the end of the curved stroke.

149. Body fragment.   Fig. 16; Pl. 13.
H 555. Altar area.
Either way.

–ΧΕ–

150. Body fragment.   Fig. 16; Pl. 13.
H 239. Votive dump.
Left to right.

–.ΥΙ–

151. Body fragment.   Fig. 16; Pl. 13.
H 544. Altar area.
Probably left to right.

–.Π–

152. Rim fragment.   Fig. 16; Pl. 13.
H 152. Altar area.
Two lines retrograde.

Line 1: ΑΙ–
Line 2: Ε–

The first letter of line 1 is probably an alpha; the surface is chipped away in the area of the crossbar.

153. Body fragments.   Fig. 16; Pl. 14.
Two non-joining fragments of the same vessel. Votive dump.

a. H 178. Left to right. –ΕΣ
b. H 159. Left to right. –ΕΑ–

154. Body fragments.   Fig. 16; Pl. 14.
Two non-joining fragments from the same vessel. Altar area.

a. H 519. Probably retrograde. –.Α–
b. H 520. Retrograde? –.ΥΙ–

155. Body fragment.   Fig. 16; Pl. 14.
H 196. Votive dump.
Either way.

–ΙΔ–

156. Body fragment.   Fig. 16; Pl. 14.
H 186. Votive dump.
The piece is now lost, and the photograph published here is an old one which shows the sherd at twice its size.
Retrograde.

–Ε.–

157. Fragmentary band handle of a one-handled cup.

H 76 (NM 16127). Votive dump. *A.J.A.* 38, 1934, p. 24, no. 20.
A single letter, chi, incised on the outer face of the handle, near the rim attachment. To the right of this is a scratch which should not be read as a letter.

158. Lower-body fragment. Fig. 16; Pl. 14.

H 528. Altar area.

Apparently complete in a single letter: A; no letters to either side. Upside down to vessel.

Single alphas are often found on objects dedicated to Athena, undoubtedly as abbreviations of the goddess' name (cf., for example, those from the sanctuary of Athena on the acropolis of Sparta: *B.S.A.* 30, 1928-1930, p. 251, fig. 6, nos. 1-11, 14, 22). Elsewhere single alphas may have some other meaning: e. g. the fourteen complete 5th century examples from Olympia, W. Schiering, *Olympische Forschungen* V, 1964, p. 156, no. 79, and the eleven from the Pnyx, G. Davidson and D. B. Thompson, *Hesperia,* Suppl. VII, *Small Objects from the Pnyx: I,* 1943, p. 29. The significance, if any, of single alpha from Hymettos is unknown.

159. Fragment from the rim and upper body. Fig. 16; Pl. 14.

H 410. Heroon.

A single preserved letter, incised with a blunt point: –A; broken away at left, no letters to right. This graffito and the following ones may be incomplete and the single letters preserved only by chance.

160. Fragment from the rim and upper body. Fig. 16; Pl. 14.

H 507. Altar area.

The single letter –A incised upside down to the vessel; to the right no letters, to the left broken away.

161. Body fragment of a cooking-ware vessel.

H 77 (NM 16131). Votive dump. *A.J.A.* 38, 1934, p. 24, no. 21.

A single letter: –A–; broken away at either side.

162. Base fragment. Fig. 16; Pl. 14.

H 143. Heroon.

The letter –T– incised upside down to the vessel; broken away at either side.

163. Body fragment. Fig. 16; Pl. 14.

H 160. Votive dump.

Part of a single letter, rho or upsilon; broken away at left, possibly not at right.

164. Body fragment. Pl. 14.

H 401. Votive dump.

Part of an epsilon, retrograde; broken away at left, no letters to right.

165. Rim fragment. Fig. 16; Pl. 15.

H 543. Altar area.
Grayish buff clay.
Part of an epsilon, left to right; broken away at either side.

166. Base fragment. Pl. 15.

H 416. Votive dump.

The single letter gamma incised on the reserved resting surface; no letters to the right, broken away to left.

SYMBOLS

167. Rim fragment of a Corinthian-type skyphos. Fig. 17; Pl. 15.

H 502. Altar area.
Fine greenish buff clay, probably Corinthian; good shiny black glaze.
Incised on the outside a tripod-cauldron, the greater part of which is preserved.
Late seventh or early sixth century B.C.

168. Upper-body fragment. Fig. 17; Pl. 15.

H 222. Votive dump.

An incised five-pointed star, partly broken off at left. A similar star scratched on a late 7th century B.C. plate from Smyrna is called an owner's or merchant's mark: L. H. Jeffery, *B.S.A.* 59, 1964, p. 40, no. 12. In the 5th century the star may have sometimes been an apotropaic symbol: cf. W. Schiering, *Olympische Forschungen* V, 1964, p. 155, no. 67, and p. 157.

169. Rim fragment. Fig. 17; Pl. 15.

H 236. Votive dump.

Part of an incised five-pointed star like **168**.

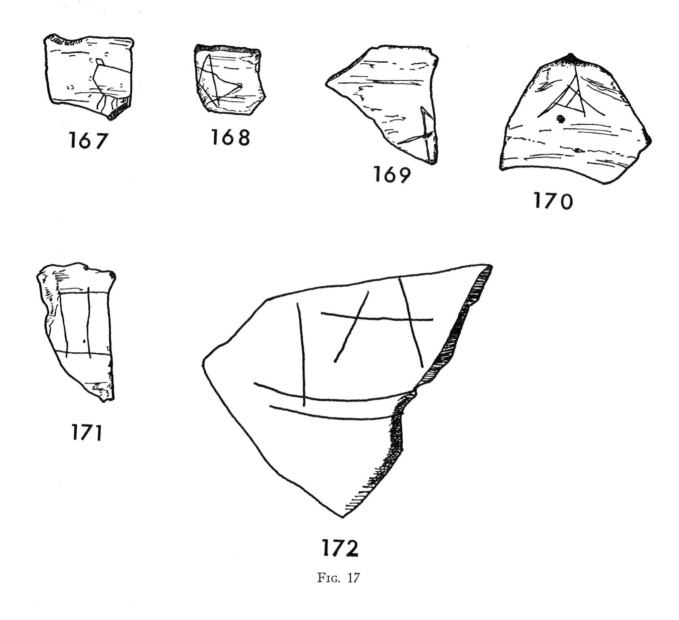

Fig. 17

170. Fragment from the lower body.

Fig. 17; Pl. 15.

H 382. Votive dump.

Apparently complete. Some kind of symbol or perhaps a ligature involving the letters alpha and delta: cf. two 6th century B.C. ligatures of these letters from the precinct of Aphaia on Aigina, A. Furtwängler, *Aegina, Das Heiligtum der Aphaia,* Munich, 1906, p. 466, nos. 367, 368.

171. Rim fragment.   Fig. 17; Pl. 15.

H 153. Altar area.

A symbol of four lines, apparently complete.

OTHER INSCRIPTIONS

172. Base fragment of a Late Roman jug.

Fig. 17; Pl. 15.

H 400. Votive dump.

Flat bottom and convex side wall. Coarse, pinkish buff clay, unglazed.

The letters –AI– (Greek?) incised on the resting surface after firing with a sharp point. Left to right?

Jugs with flat bottoms are very late in the Roman period: cf. *Agora* V, pl. 35, the jugs from Group N.

Early seventh century after Christ.

173. Inscription on stone.   Pl. 15.

H 144. West of Heroon on surface. *A.J.A.* 44, 1940, p. 3; *S.E.G.* XIII, 37. Length 0.688 m.; Width 0.322 m.; Thickness 0.09 m.; Letter height 0.11 m.

Thin, rough slab of hard, gray limestone. Upper, lower, and left sides roughly smooth, right side broken away; inscribed face smooth, back face rough.

In center of slab, running left to right, the letters HEP– are shallowly gouged out with a rough implement. The inscription is broken away at the right; below the preserved letters and to the right are traces of a curved letter, omicron or theta.

R. S. Young has plausibly suggested that the letters may be part of the name Herakles. That or ℎέρ[οος – –] seem the two best possibilities.

Seventh century B.C.?

THE GRAFFITI AND THE BEGINNING OF WRITING IN ATTICA

FORMS AND VALUES OF THE LETTERS

The graffiti from Mount Hymettos range in date from the beginning of the 7th to the early 6th century B.C. Not only the forms of the letters but also certain inconsistencies in their usage strongly suggest that the inscribers were inexperienced in the art of writing and that the alphabet was new to Attica and still in a state of flux at that time. Had writing been known for even fifty years prior to the dedication of the inscribed Hymettos cups, one might expect to see them exhibiting neater and more regularly formed letters and a more standard usage in their shape and value. But one need merely to glance at their straggling and uneven letter forms to be convinced that they must stand near the beginning of Attic writing.

Such remarks on the primitive appearance of the Hymettos letter forms are quite in contrast to the observations made by Professor Blegen, who wrote that they were not so primitive.[12] But his comparison was with the letters on the Dipylon oinochoe, which, if Jeffery is correct, were not written by an Athenian. The Hymettos letter forms do appear advanced alongside those on the Dipylon jug, but when compared with later Attic graffiti they look very archaic. A brief discussion of the Hymettos letter forms and values will be helpful, not only in demonstrating to

[12] *A.J.A.* 38, 1934, p. 26.

what extent they differ from those in the later Attic alphabet but also in showing to what degree individual letters were influenced by other local Greek scripts.[13]

The letter alpha occurs with equal frequency in its two usual archaic forms: α2 with the second leg somewhat curved, and α3 with both legs straight and the crossbar slanted, usually downward to the direction of writing. The letter is usually upright, but in two instances, **70** and **71**, it is tilted, almost sidelong. Other letters in these two inscriptions are also tilted, however, so the shape of the alpha is probably the result of the handwriting style of the inscribers rather than a harkening back to earlier forms such as are present on the Dipylon oinochoe or in Phoenician inscriptions.[14]

Beta appears with both curved and angular loops. β1 and β2, the common early types in which the loops do not join at the center, are found in **20**, **21**, and **51**. **43** and **52** contain the normal β3. The Corinthian and Cretan forms of beta are not present.

Gamma is always represented in its normal Attic isosceles form: **1**, **10**, **20**, **21**, **27-33**, **35**, **36**, **57-59**, **63**, **67**, **71**, **74**, **83**, **86**, **88**, **109**, **138**, **140**, **145**, and **166**. The Euboian lunate gamma is not represented.

Although δ1 is described by Jeffery as abnormal, it occurs frequently enough on the Hymettos sherds to deserve consideration as a normal early form: **1-5**, **8**, **16**, **29**, **36**, **38**, **46**, **50**, **53**, **55-57**, and **110**. The regular δ2 occurs in **1**, **7**, **9**, *30*, **49**, **57**, **58**, **73**, **128**, and **145**. The form common in Boiotia and Euboia, with one of the diagonals curved, is found in **20**, but it is probably the result of a slip of the writing implement.

For the letter digamma, see **20**.

The letter zeta is not preserved in any of these graffiti.

The aspirate heta is present in both the closed (Ⱶ 1) and open (Ⱶ 2) forms. Ⱶ 1, the earlier form, occurs in **1**, **13**, **27**, **47**, **48**, **55**, **60**, and **114**. Ⱶ 2 occurs six times: in **2**, **3**, twice in **9**, **66**, and **73**. In **2** and **73** the letter cannot be the aspirate but must have the value of a vowel. In **9**, if Young's explanation is correct, the letter is used as both aspirate and long vowel. Since only the psilotic dialects of Ionia and Crete gave a phonetic value to this letter, its appearance here as both aspirate and long vowel is significant, because it suggests that at this time the Attic alphabet was still being formulated. For during its initial stages a new alphabet is easily influenced by more established ones. This is most often seen in the shapes and values of the

---

[13] In the discussion of letter forms which follows, α1, β1, etc. refer to Miss Jeffery's chart of Attic letter forms, *L.S.A.G.*, p. 66, fig. 26.

[14] The sidelong alphas of the Dipylon oinochoe are harder to explain. They resemble Phoenician *'alep* but in reverse. How the Greek upright form developed out of these prototypes is difficult to guess. If Jeffery's hypothetical alpha 2 (*L.S.A.G.*, p. 23) did in fact exist, then perhaps the development was somewhat along the lines suggested by B. Einarson in *Class. Phil.* 62, 1967, p. 17, note 2.

new alphabet's letters. A certain letter may be shaped in different ways or have more than one phonetic value as a result of differing outside influences. Gradually, each letter of the new alphabet is standardized into one form with one phonetic value. Here, the letter heta appears to be a good illustration of this process. Except for the Hymettos examples, there are few other occurrences of heta used as a vowel in inscriptions written in the Attic alphabet except for 5th century B.C. inscriptions in which Ionicisms begin to appear. Thus, early in its history the Attic heta reveals foreign influence, in this case Ionic. But since the Attic and Ionic dialects were basically different in several respects, Ionic usages, such as heta = long vowel, were soon rejected. The Ionic element then disappears, leaving no traces in the developed Attic alphabet.[15]

The circular letters, theta and omicron, are invariably very small in proportion to the other letters and often quite irregularly shaped. These traits illustrate the great difficulty encountered in incising circular letters on hard surfaces. Later graffiti, from the 6th century B.C. onward, generally exhibit more regularly shaped circular letters. Omicron occurs very frequently, while the examples of theta are θ1 in **12, 19, 43, 45, 64,** and **80,** and θ2 in **13, 17, 41, 44,** and **59.** There are no examples of θ3. In **11** the theta is a square instead of a circle, and in **14** the letter has only one internal stroke, the horizontal.

The letter iota is always a straight vertical stroke. There is no evidence among the Hymettos graffiti that the Attic script ever possessed the Corinthian or Cretan broken forms. Broken iota occurs in only one inscription in Attica, on the Dipylon oinochoe. **6** has an iota which appears to be broken, but only because it crosses an unevenness of the surface.

The letter kappa is usually written in the early form κ1: **13, 15, 36, 73, 83, 136.** In two instances, **9** and **11,** the transverse bars do not join the vertical at the same point, and in two others, **66** and **141,** they meet slightly behind the vertical.

λ1 is the common Ionic lambda, occurring only rarely in Attic inscriptions. **9** definitely contains λ1, and **26** and **52** very probably so. The use here of Ionic lambda is another indication of Ionic influence in the early Attic alphabet. The Ionic form was rejected after a short period of use, however, probably because of its confusion with Attic gamma. Normal λ2 is found in **22, 34, 36, 37, 43, 50, 51, 56, 60, 70, 71, 76, 79, 84, 85,** and **147.**

Mu is always written with four strokes: **2, 4, 22, 29, 36, 39, 41, 50, 59, 63, 64, 78, 89, 95, 100, 101, 104, 108, 123,** and **125.** The five-stroked mu of Eretria and Crete does not occur.

The examples of pi are regularly shaped: **19, 26, 27, 34, 36, 42, 49, 56, 58,**

---

[15] This is not the only course taken by the letter heta in the Greek scripts. Rhodes and Paros, for example, used both the open and closed forms for the aspirate heta as well as the long vowel eta. Various other states settled on other combinations which allowed them to retain a long vowel eta while also using an aspirate. See Jeffery, *L.S.A.G.,* pp. 28-29.

62, 66, 75, 78, 106, 113, 116, 121, 126, and **151**. No examples of the Cretan lunate form occur.

The letter koppa occurs twice, in **54** and **144**.

Rho, in its two usual archaic forms, is found in **1, 18, 19, 26-29, 31-35, 42, 44, 49, 50, 53, 55, 57, 58, 63, 82, 107, 124**, and **148**. There are no examples of legless or tailed rho, except **148** where the tail is probably a slip of the writing instrument.

The letter sigma occurs frequently in its normal form (σ1) with three strokes: **3, 4, 6, 10, 27-30, 34, 36, 37, 40, 41, 47, 58, 66, 72, 75, 77, 78, 81, 91-94, 120, 130** and **153**. The Ionic four-stroked sigma (σ2) is found in **1, 2, 5, 54, 65, 80, 98, 100**, and **119**.[16]

Upsilon is found in **18, 23, 30, 34, 36, 39, 45-47, 54, 56, 61, 68, 69, 108, 117, 136, 145, 147**, and **150**, always in the early form v1.

The examples of ϕ1 are **27, 28, 34, 50**, and **112**. ϕ2 is found in **38** and **48**. ϕ3 does not occur.

The letter chi occurs as χ1 in **26, 50, 63, 74, 88, 105, 124, 149**, and **157**, and as χ2 in **1, 23, 53**, and **80**. In only two cases, **1** and **53**, can its phonetic value be determined with certainty as *kh*, but it is unlikely that in any of the others it represents xi.

Xi, psi, and omega, which have no place in the established Attic alphabet, are not found in any of the Hymettos inscriptions. The combination of chi plus sigma which represents xi is perhaps present in **54**. Phi plus sigma for psi would have occurred in all of the ἔγραφσε inscriptions, but the combination is preserved only once, in **27**.

In the case of three of the letters discussed above, heta, lambda, and sigma, Ionic forms not used in the standard Attic alphabet were seen to have been in wider use in the formative Attic script than previously thought. It has been argued that such a situation would exist only during an alphabet's initial stages of formation, and that afterwards the script would be more standardized and less receptive to foreign usage. Thus, the Hymettos graffiti must belong to an early stage in the history of Attic writing. In view of the provincial nature of the sanctuary in which they were found, it is highly unlikely that the documents containing non-Attic features were written by foreigners and not Attic citizens. It is much more probable that they reveal phenomena of the formative Attic alphabet, which reflect the uncertainty and development that preceded standardization.

Another indication that the Hymettos graffiti stand near the beginning of writing in Attica is the general archaic look of the lettering. It is often tall and spidery, and characterized by long, curving tails and small circles. This agrees well with the

---

[16] An inscribed sherd from the Hymettos site now in the topographical sherd collection of the German Archaeological Institute in Athens also contains a four-stroked sigma: cf. *Ath. Mitt.* 87, 1972, p. 280, abb. 1. I was able to examine this sherd, a base fragment of a Phaleron cup, and others from the Hymettos site, through the kindness of Professor Brommer.

lettering of the earliest extant inscriptions from other parts of Greece, e. g. the dedication of Mantiklos on a bronze statuette from Boiotia and the graffito of Korakos on a cup from Rhodes, both of which date around 700 B.C.[17] Later graffiti executed when writing was more familiar generally exhibit less straggling and straighter letters. Two of the inscribed Hymettos cups which show the contrast between these lettering styles, **36** and **50**, are fairly complete and can be dated closely. **50**, with tall, curving letters, is inscribed on a cup belonging to the early 7th century, while the cup bearing inscription **36**, with small, neat letters, can be assigned to the third quarter of the 7th century. Some inscribed Subgeometric cups from the Athenian Agora which are stratigraphically datable confirm this letter-form development. Brann S 17 and S 18, cups of the second quarter of the 7th century, have inscriptions which exhibit all of the early features of **50**, while the lettering of the inscriptions on Brann F 38 and G 33, cups of the third and final quarters of the 7th century, is small and neat like **36**.

None of the other Hymettos graffiti on Subgeometric fragments can be dated more closely in the 7th century B.C., but taking into account the almost unanimous evidence of the lettering style of other early inscriptions from Attica and other areas of Greece, it seems reasonable to conclude that the Hymettos graffiti with tall, straggling letters are to be dated early in the 7th century, probably not too long after the practice of writing first began in Attica.[18] Some might contend that the archaic appearance of the letters of some of the Hymettos inscriptions is due more to the inexperience of individual inscribers than to the general immaturity of the Attic alphabet.[19] This does not seem to be a valid argument, however, since almost all Attic graffiti which date before 650 B.C. are crudely done. In other words, everyone was inexperienced in writing at that time because the alphabet itself was new.

It is interesting to note the large number of Hymettos inscriptions with left to right directional writing, almost half the total. Early single-line Greek inscriptions usually read from right to left, since the Near Eastern sources from which the Greeks acquired the alphabet wrote that way. The practice of writing in a left to right direction was gradually evolved by the Greeks in the 7th century B.C. Owing

---

[17] The Mantiklos statuette: Jeffery, *L.S.A.G.*, p. 94, no. 1; Korakos' cup: *ibid.*, p. 356, no. 1.

[18] A note of caution must be injected into any discussion of the epigraphical style of early graffiti. Rhys Carpenter, in a review of Jeffery's *Local Scripts* (*A.J.P.* 84, 1963, pp. 83-85), argued that " Nestor's cup " from Pithekussai threatened to imperil the dating of early inscriptions by epigraphic style because the letters of the inscription on the cup looked so much more advanced than the cup itself. But the inscription and the cup have been shown indisputably to be contemporary (H. Metzger, *Rev. Et. Anc.* 67, 1965, pp. 301-305). In any consideration of style such as this one, exceptions, sometimes marked ones, are bound to occur. Carpenter overstated his case, and we need not view " Nestor's cup " as fatal to our discussion of early lettering style. Now see the commendable remarks of A. J. Graham on the subject: *Acta of the Fifth International Congress of Greek and Latin Epigraphy, Cambridge, 1967*, Oxford, 1971, pp. 9-17.

[19] John Boardman believes this may be the case even for the Dipylon oinochoe: cf. *B.S.A.* 49, 1954, p. 185 and note 10.

to the fragmentary state of the Hymettos documents we cannot determine whether those written left to right occur on cups mainly from later in the 7th century or whether they range throughout the century. We can only say that sometime before 600 B.C. the practice of writing in a left to right direction had become just as common as retrograde writing. By the early 6th century inscriptions written right to left were exceptional in Attica, occurring only in special circumstances or written by senior citizens who were accustomed to writing retrograde.[20]

CONTEXT AND CONTENT

Some of the Hymettos inscriptions were scratched on sherds. A prime example of this is **2**, a fragment of a closed pot. The dedication " to Zeus Semios " is inscribed on the unglazed inside. Thus the pot was already broken when the inscriber picked up the sherd and scratched his dedication. Now a single, broken potsherd would seem to be a quite unlikely gift to dedicate to a deity. A sample of writing, on the other hand, might not have been considered so inappropriate, especially if writing was a new and highly regarded art at the time. The worshipper would believe that a specimen of this new skill which allowed him to express in visible and permanent form that which not so long before he could only think or say verbally was a most worthy gift. In the case of **2** the fact that the dedication happened to be on a mere sherd mattered little: it was the writing itself which was the gift.[21]

What some of the Hymettos inscriptions actually say is in itself a strong indication that writing was a new skill when the cups were inscribed. The verb form ἔγραφσε occurs several times, and because we are dealing with simple, glazed vessels, the word cannot refer to painting, but must instead mean " so-and-so himself wrote it." In other words writing must have been still so new that its accomplishment was being stressed.

Another manner in which a votary could display his knowledge of writing was by scratching the alphabet. Throughout antiquity people practiced their writing ability by incising abecedaria on pieces of pottery. But only at a time when writing itself was new would abecedaria have been considered appropriate dedications for a deity. They do not find their way into sanctuaries of the 6th century B.C. or later because by then writing had lost its novelty. The same may be said for the ἔγραφσε inscriptions. The accomplishment of writing is never stressed among dedications found in later sanctuaries.

It has been suggested by others that the language of some of the Hymettos inscriptions might indicate that the art of writing had been known in Attica for some time

[20] See the discussion by Jeffery, *L.S.A.G.*, pp. 47-48.
[21] A few other graffiti, placed upside down to their respective vessels, may also have been inscribed on sherds: **44**, **52**, **69**, **81**, **94**, **101**, **131**, **136**, **137**, **160**, **162**. Perhaps also inscribed on sherds were **115** and **116**, which run sideways to their respective vessels, **7**, on the inside of a rim fragment, and **166**, on a base fragment.

previously.[22] In certain cases, such as **36** and **49**, the message is obscene or trivial. This is taken to presuppose a long period of development. But obscenity is no proof of advanced literacy.[23] These inscriptions should rather be viewed as the products of precocious minds who, having but recently learned to write, were already cursing their enemies and toasting their friends on their drinking vessels. In any case, the general appearance of the letter forms and the emphasis placed on the act of writing are more compelling reasons for believing that the Hymettos inscriptions stand near the beginning of writing in Attica, not following a long period of development.

SOURCE AND DATE OF INTRODUCTION OF THE ATTIC ALPHABET

If the inscriptions on pottery from Mount Hymettos can be accepted as belonging to a very early stage in the history of Attic writing, perhaps a few worthwhile remarks may be made concerning the date of introduction of the alphabet to Attica and the possible source from which it came. We have seen, through the evidence of the Dipylon oinochoe, that the local population was aware of alphabetic writing as early as 740 B.C. The time was ripe for them to learn their letters, and the Hymettos graffiti show that by the early 7th century this had been accomplished. A short period of development, perhaps not more than one generation, must have preceded these documents. So the last quarter of the 8th century may be taken as roughly the period during which the first Attic citizens learned the proper use of the alphabet.

We need not look far to discover who their teacher was. Several of the letter forms suggest Ionic influence while only the lack of xi, psi, and omega would deny it. On the other hand, influence from other areas is more often denied. Attic gamma denies Corinthian and Euboian influence; beta, lambda, and sigma deny Corinthian and island influence; epsilon denies Corinthian influence, and chi Euboian influence. All of this suggests direct contact with Ionia, not via Euboia, the Cyclades, Crete, or Corinth. In fact we could readily conclude that Attic merchant-traders introduced the alphabet into Attica directly from Ionia, were it not for the evidence of Attica's increasing provincialism during the 8th century B.C. There is a marked decline in Attic overseas activity, especially after 750 B.C., the very time when Attic citizens were learning about alphabet writing.[24] If this evidence is a true indication of the situation, i.e. that Attic traders were not active at that time in the literate states of Ionia or the Near East, we should therefore envisage the reverse, Ionic Greek traders introducing the alphabet into Attica.

[22] A. Blakeway, *J.R.S.* 25, 1935, p. 143, note 54; J. Forsdyke, *Greece Before Homer,* London, 1956, p. 19.

[23] An early graffito from the Athenian Agora, Brann S 18, is probably another obscene vituperation. It is on a cup which dates half a century before the Hymettos vituperative inscription **36**, and it further demonstrates that the subjects of even the earliest written documents were not confined to niceties.

[24] See *Agora* VIII, pp. 27-28, and Coldstream, *G.G.P.*, pp. 360-362.

Two of Attica's neighbors, Euboia and Aigina, provide a possible alternative source for the Attic alphabet. As revealed by continuing discoveries of early inscriptions, these two states acquired literacy at an early date, perhaps even before Attica. At Lefkandi, possibly the site of Old Eretria, three graffito sherds were found in Late Geometric contexts,[25] and excavations at the Euboian colony of Pithekussai (Ischia) have uncovered several very early documents probably written by immigrants who learned the alphabet in Euboia itself.[26] From Aigina a dipinto on a fragment of a votive plaque dating before 720 B.C. probably demonstrates that island's very early literacy.[27] Unlike Attica, however, these states were leaders in commercial trade with the East in the late 8th century B.C., and their merchants may well have learned the alphabet at foreign ports and brought it back to their respective homes.[28]

Attica was, then, flanked on either side by literate states with whom she frequently came into contact. Her dealings with Euboia were friendly and plentiful, while those with Aigina, perhaps a politically hostile neighbor, were undoubtedly numerous in the area of commerce, since Attic merchants produced many of the goods sought by the East, and Aigina possessed the ships needed to transport them. Ceramic evidence confirms increasing Attic-Aiginetan contact in the latter part of the 8th century B.C.[29]

The early Euboian and Aiginetan scripts are not so well known as the Attic, so it is difficult to assess the influence of one upon the others. But the Hymettos graffiti do tend, as we have seen, to deny Euboian influence. On the other hand the Attic alphabet is very close to the Aiginetan. Thus it may have been that Aigina acted as an intermediary between Attica and Ionia in the transmission of the alphabet.

[25] See *Excavations at Lefkandi, Euboea: 1964-66* (edd. M. Popham and L. Sackett), London, 1968, pp. 33-34.

[26] " Nestor's cup ", from the second half of the 8th century B.C.: G. Buchner and C. Russo, *Rend. Linc.* 10, 1955, pp. 215-234; a sherd with a sidelong alpha from before 725 B.C.: M. Guarducci, *Epigrafia Greca*, I, Rome, 1967, p. 225, no. 5; a Late Geometric krater fragment with a dipinto: G. Buchner, *Arch. Reports for 1970-71*, p. 67.

[27] See J. Boardman, *B.S.A.* 49, 1954, pp. 183-186. Boardman believes that the plaque was made and painted in Athens rather than on Aigina. He argues that the painted letter forms on the fragment are advanced and presuppose a generation or more of familiarity with the practice of writing. But he fails to take into consideration the fact that a painted inscription will invariably appear more developed than a contemporary incised example. For more on this, see Jeffery, *L.S.A.G.*, pp. 63-65.

[28] For Euboian activity in the literate East at Al Mina during the 8th century B.C., see J. Boardman, *The Greeks Overseas*, Baltimore and London, 1964, pp. 62-66. For Aigina there is no comparable direct evidence, but we may infer from her early history that her merchant ships were in contact with the East (Herodotos, V, 83).

[29] Coldstream, *G.G.P.*, p. 361, note 10, notes the total absence of Attic Late Geometric IB pottery from Aigina; Attic pottery begins to be found in some quantity on the island at the beginning of the Late Geometric II period (*ca.* 735 B.C.).

Much more early epigraphical evidence from Aigina is needed, however, before this possibility can really be investigated.

LITERACY

The Hymettos inscriptions have some bearing on the question of the extent of literacy in Attica in the Archaic period. They suggest that literacy was somewhat more widespread, at least in western Attica, by the end of the 7th century B.C. than heretofore generally supposed. Considering the scarcity of contemporary evidence it is difficult to determine the place of the Hymettos inscriptions in the development of Attic literacy, but it would surely be wrong to believe that they formed, when dedicated, a unique group of documents. They must instead be representative of the fairly wide extent of literacy which developed during the first century after the introduction of the alphabet. This means more than just the ability to write one's name. It requires that a man be able to express himself in writing with a minimum of difficulty, and that he be able to read almost anything put before him. The large series of Acropolis dedications and ostraka from Athens confirm the prevalence of literacy for the 6th and 5th centuries, and the Hymettos inscriptions do the same, I feel, for the 7th century.[30] This is not to claim that everyone in early Athens and its environs could read and write, but it seems likely to me that by the end of the 7th century there were as many literate citizens as illiterate.

H. L. Lorimer also believed that the Hymettos graffiti indicated a fairly widespread ability to read and write,[31] but while I agree with her general conclusion, I hesitate to adopt her reasons. She suggested that the subject matter of the Hymettos graffiti and the cheapness of the vases on which they are inscribed point to general literacy. The vessels themselves do not necessarily indicate this. It is interesting to note that very few pieces of the finest Protoattic pottery are inscribed. The impression is that whether the knowledge of writing was widespread or the possession of a relatively few people, plain cups and skyphoi would be favored for writing. Perhaps the reason for this was that the more elaborate pottery of the 7th century was produced mainly for ceremonial use in graves, while the plain wares were the everyday vessels of literate and illiterate alike and were thus more plentiful and readily available for inscribing. As for the subject matter, just as it is no sign of advanced literacy, it is also not a sign of general literacy.

Thus, it is not from any kind of internal evidence that we can judge the degree of literacy represented by the Hymettos inscriptions. Rather, it is the very fact of their existence which compels us to accord to 7th century Attic citizenry more than just a feeble ability to read and write.

[30] I cannot agree with the arguments of E. A. Havelock that Attica did not really emerge from a semi-literate condition until the end of the 5th century B.C.: *Preface to Plato,* Oxford, 1963, pp. 36-60, and *Prologue to Greek Literacy,* Semple Lecture Series, University of Cincinnati, 1971.

[31] *Homer and the Monuments,* London, 1950, p. 129, note 2.

THE GRAFFITI AND THE SANCTUARY

THE DEDICATORY LANGUAGE [32]

We have seen that the Hymettos dedications differ somewhat from the written dedications of other sanctuaries.[33] Not even large groups of dedicatory inscriptions from early sanctuaries such as Perachora or Emporio on Chios contain any abecedaria or ἔγραφσε inscriptions. On the other hand, many of the Hymettos graffiti consist of common dedicatory phrases which differ little from those of other sanctuaries. The vessel dedicated sometimes speaks in the first person, announcing that it belongs to the deity: εἰμὶ τō Διός. In other cases the worshipper writes that he is dedicating the vase to the god: ὁ δεῖνα ἀνέθεκε τōι Δί. The vocative of the deity's name, which is found occasionally among dedications of other sanctuaries, does not occur here.

Concerning the nature of the symbols not much can be said. Symbols are not often found among sanctuary dedications, but when they are, they are most often explained as magic symbols.[34] The examples from Hymettos are possibly of this

nature, or, as suggested above, they could be some sort of owners' marks.

IDENTIFICATION AND DATE OF THE SANCTUARY

The identification of the site was discussed in the preceding chapter. The inscribed fragments with the word ἀνέθεκε and those mentioning Zeus give proof in writing that the site on the summit of Mount Hymettos was a sanctuary, and that it was sacred to Zeus.

The sanctuary had a long life before the inscribed dedications were made, as is documented by the great quantity of Protogeometric and Geometric pottery found in the votive dump. Inscribed dedications begin to be made no earlier than 700 B.C., and continue through to the end of the 7th and beginning of the 6th centuries B.C. From the late 7th century are **1**, scratched on an early black-figured pot, and **13**, on the base of an early Corinthian alabastron. From the early 6th century come **33**, **94**, **126**, and **167**, on fragments of black-glazed skyphoi and kylikes.[35] These are the latest inscribed dedications found at the site. Afterwards, occasional offerings seem to have been made, as some later pottery was found in the dump. But the graffito sherds indicate that regular visits to the sanctuary ceased after the early 6th century B.C.

[32] For an excellent treatment of the language and function of pot dedications, see Karl Lehmann, *Samothrace, 2*, II, *The Inscriptions on Ceramics and Minor Objects*, New York, 1960.

[33] For a selected bibliography of major groups of sanctuary graffiti, see Karl Lehmann, *op. cit.* (note 32, above), p. 4, note 5.

[34] A notable exception is Perachora where 35 trade inscriptions were found, dating from the 6th to the 4th century B.C.; L. H. Jeffery, *Perachora* II, Oxford, 1962, pp. 399-400, nos. 131-165.

[35] For the types of vessels to which these fragments belong, see *Agora* XII: the 6th century Corinthian-type skyphos, pp. 81-83; early kylikes, pp. 88-89. **94** may belong to an early Komast cup; **33** may be a bit later.

CHAPTER III

THE POTTERY AND OTHER FINDS

No meaningful stratification could be detected by the excavators in the depression on the summit of Mount Hymettos. A great mass of pottery, including many complete vessels, was recovered and found to range widely in date. The sherds and more complete vessels were thoroughly jumbled, however, so that even at the deepest levels of excavation Classical sherds and Roman lamp fragments were invariably found alongside Geometric and Subgeometric material. The pottery was concentrated mainly at the north end of the depression, opposite the rectangular foundation above and to the west, which is conjectured to have been the altar of Zeus. The proximity of the pottery mass to this foundation suggests that the depression served as a dump for dedications discarded from the altar above.

The sanctuary was in use for a very long time. As a result the depression filled gradually, as old dedications were periodically gathered from around the altar and scattered in the dump. This would explain the lack of stratification. There would be no real silting-in on top of the mountain where earth is scarce anyway, and no layer of pottery would have had a chance to be buried with earth before later material was thrown into its midst. If, as seems to be the case, both altar and depression were in use during the Late Roman period, then the Roman lamps can be accounted for in the same way.[1] There was no evidence of any late building in the depression which could have confused the stratification or have been responsible for the presence of the late lamps. Instead, the dump must have lain fairly exposed, and the Roman material must represent the remains of dedications, just like the Geometric and Subgeometric pottery before it.

The curved foundation in the depression (Fig. 3), probably the remains of a stone-lined pit, has been mentioned previously. Numbers of pots, stacked and in rows, were found within the foundation, but the confusion of pottery was too great to allow the excavators to determine when the pit was actually constructed or for how long it was used. It was probably built during the Geometric period and used for the storage of votives.

Offerings were made over a period of several centuries, thus giving us a great wealth of material from which to draw in writing a history of the sanctuary. In the following pages, however, only a selection of the pottery and other finds will be presented. In view of the lack of stratification and the occurrence of large numbers

---

[1] In this study " Late Roman " is used in a chronological sense to include the 4th through the 7th centuries after Christ.

of duplicates, as well as the fact that in general the pottery is undistinguished, cheap ware, it hardly seems worth while to make the selection very large. Therefore, only pieces which represent a particular time period or are of interest in themselves will be included.[2]

CATALOGUE

The catalogue is meant to supplement the photographs. The description of obvious details of shape and painted design are therefore generally omitted. Breakages, missing parts, and restorations are not usually noted unless they significantly affect the profile.

CLAY. Most of the Geometric and Subgeometric pottery from the Hymettos sanctuary can be described as Attic fine ware.[3] The fabric of vessels from other areas will be described under particular entries.

GLAZE. The paint of the Hymettos pots is generally of good quality and well preserved. The color ranges through various shades of red, brown, and black and will be stated in such terms in the catalogue. The advantages of using a more precise authority than one's own subjective eye for describing the color of both glaze and clay is recognized, though no such aid was available for this study.[4]

DATING. Since there was no meaningful stratification in the dump, no objects can be dated by context. Instead, each piece is assigned to a broad chronological period on the basis of style and similarity to published parallels. Heavy reliance has been made on the fine study collection of pottery in the Agora Museum. For the Geometric pottery the tripartite division of the Attic Geometric period is used. Each object is assigned to as narrow a sub-division as possible, although in a great many cases only the broader divisions could be used with confidence.

---

[2] A select inventory of vessels, following the same principle, was made by Young just after World War II. I have used his inventory as the basis of my selection besides adding to it slightly. Most of the catalogued vessels have numerous duplicates or close parallels among the uninventoried material. A certain amount of material could not be taken into account. This includes an unknown quantity lost during and after the war and several tins of sherds reburied at the site after the war. Furthermore, I did not have the opportunity to examine several small groups of sherds from the Hymettos excavations known by me to be in private collections, nor two small groups of vessels presented by the Greek government to museums in America: one to the Metropolitan Museum of Art in New York, cf. *Bull. Metr. Mus.* 26, 1931, p. 23, and G. M. A. Richter, *Handbook of the Greek Collection*, Cambridge, Mass., 1953, p. 26, pl. 16, g, i; the other to the University of California at Berkeley. I am indebted to Stella Grobel Miller for bringing this latter group to my attention.

[3] Cf. *Agora* VIII, pp. 29-30. But whether it is Athenian or not is another matter. E. L. Smithson previously thought that the Hymettos pottery might just be bad Athenian work: cf. *Hesperia* 30, 1961, p. 155, note 16. She tells me that she is now not so certain. A more definite statement on the origin of the Hymettos pottery must await proper scientific studies of the clay of Geometric pottery from Athens and outlying areas.

[4] See *Thorikos* III, pp. 109-113, for an explanation of the use of the *Munsell Soil Color Chart* for such purposes.

ABBREVIATIONS:

AE ......Bronze.
diam. .....diameter.
dim. ......dimension.
E.G. ......Early Geometric.
est. ......estimated.
F.M. .....Furumark Motif Number in A. Furumark, *The Mycenaean Pottery,* Stockholm, 1941.
F.S. ......Furumark Shape Number.
H. ....Height.

L. ....Length.
L.G. .....Late Geometric.
L.H. .....Late Helladic.
m. ....meter.
max. .....maximum.
M.G. .....Middle Geometric.
NM ......National Museum, Athens.
P. ....Preserved.
rest. ......restored.
Th. ......Thickness.
W. ....Width.

EARLY HELLADIC

174. Sauceboat.   Pl. 16.

H 380. Rest. H. to rim 0.12 m.

Base, handle and spout restored. Rim sherd at back shows the handle to have been vertical.

Handmade of fine, brownish buff clay; thick, creamy slip all over, sloppily applied, and worn.

MIDDLE HELLADIC

175. Ladle.   Pl. 16.

H 444. H. of bowl 0.062 m.

Hemispherical bowl, rounded at the bottom.

Coarse, tan-buff clay, slightly micaceous and containing red and white grit; faint traces of thin, dull red paint all over.

The bowls of other Middle Helladic ladles are usually flattened underneath or have a ring foot: cf. C. W. Blegen, *Korakou, A Prehistoric Settlement near Corinth,* Boston and New York, 1921, p. 19, fig. 26.

176. Goblet fragment, Yellow Minyan.
                    Fig. 18; Pl. 16.

H 600. P.H. 0.063 m.

Angular profile.

Fine, light yellowish buff clay, gray at core; soapy texture.

From a two-handled stemmed goblet like C. W. Blegen, *Prosymna, the Helladic Settlement Preceding the Argive Heraeum* II, Cambridge, Mass., 1937, fig. 640.

LATE HELLADIC

177. Body fragment of a Vapheio cup (F.S. 224).   Fig. 18; Pl. 16.

H 601. P.H. 0.031 m.

Preserves part of the ridge which customarily encircles the body, and the lower body zone beneath, which is decorated with painted horizontal bands; inside unglazed.

Grayish buff clay; shiny brownish black glaze. Cf. C. W. Blegen, *Prosymna* I, pp. 398-399. L.H. I.

178. Base fragment of an alabastron.   Pl. 16.

H 602. Max. dim. 0.055 m.

Resting surface decorated with a complicated form of " wheel " pattern; inside unglazed.

Fine, pinkish buff clay; dull reddish brown glaze.
L.H. II.

179. Body fragment of a piriform jar.   Pl. 16.

H 603. Max. dim. 0.065 m.

Decorated with a deep wavy line (F.M. 53); unglazed inside.

Coarse, reddish clay with white grit, possibly non-Attic; dull brown glaze.
Cf. E. French, *B.S.A.* 59, 1964, p. 247.
L.H. IIIA.

180. Fragment of a stirrup jar.   Pl. 16.

H 604. Max. dim. 0.065 m.

Fragment from the body and beginning of

shoulder. Concentric arcs (F.M. 44) in zone on body; plain inside.

Fine clay, pinkish buff at surface, tan buff at core; shiny red glaze.

Cf. E. French, *B.S.A.* 60, 1965, p. 193; *B.S.A.* 62, 1967, p. 182.

L.H. IIIA 2–IIIB 1.

183. Stem of a kylix. Pl. 17.

H 614. P.H. 0.07 m.

A painted kylix stem, broken at both ends before base and bowl. Four broad painted bands on stem.

Gray clay, burnt; brown glaze.

L.H. IIIB.

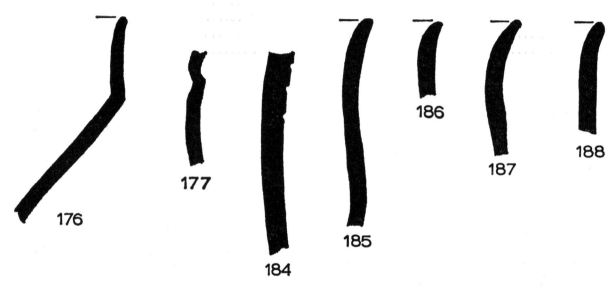

FIG. 18

181. Handle fragment of a krater (F.S. 7-9). Pl. 17.

H 613. W. of handle 0.06 m.

Fragment of applied vertical strap handle and part of the body. On outside of handle two broad glaze bands at edges.

Tan to pinkish buff clay; red to brown glaze.

Cf. K. A. Wardle, *B.S.A.* 64, 1969, pp. 270-272.

L.H. IIIA 2–IIIB 1.

182. Kylix (F.S. 274). Pl. 16.

H 489. H. 0.173 m.

Both handles restored.

Brownish buff clay with black grit; unpainted.

Cf. S. A. Immerwahr, *The Athenian Agora,* XIII, *The Neolithic and Bronze Ages,* Princeton, 1971, p. 252, nos. 433-435, p. 260, no. 473.

L.H. IIIB.

184. Body fragment of a mug (F.S. 226). Fig. 18; Pl. 17.

H 612. Max. dim. 0.063 m.

Three impressed grooves and traces of a painted decoration.

Tan buff clay.

Cf. K. A. Wardle, *B.S.A.* 64, 1969, p. 272.

L.H. IIIA 2–IIIB 1.

185. Rim fragment of a deep bowl (F.S. 284). Fig. 18; Pl. 16.

H 605. P.H. 0.052 m.; est. rim diam. 0.16 m.

A vertical wavy line (F.M. 53). Top of rim glazed; inside plain except for a band below rim.

Clay pinkish buff at core, brownish buff at surface; dark brown glaze.

THE POTTERY AND OTHER FINDS

Both **185** and **186** are Group A deep bowls:
cf. E. French, *B.S.A.* 64, 1969, pp. 74-75.
L.H. IIIB.

186. Rim fragment of a deep bowl (F.S. 284).
Fig. 18; Pl. 16.

H 606. P.H. 0.025 m.; est. rim diam. 0.10 m.

Vertical zigzag between straight vertical lines
(F.M. 75); inside plain except for a narrow
band below rim.

Light brown clay; shiny orangish red glaze.
L.H. IIIB.

187. Rim fragment of a deep bowl (F.S. 284).
Fig. 18; Pl. 16.

H 607. P.H. 0.04 m.; est. rim diam. 0.14 m.

Wide-flaring rim. Wide band at rim outside;
monochrome inside.

Tan-buff clay; brown glaze outside, thick
reddish brown inside.

From a deep bowl like *B.S.A.* 25, 1921-1923,
pl. 5, c-f.

L.H. IIIC.

188. Rim fragment of a deep bowl (F.S. 284).
Fig. 18; Pl. 16.

H 608. P.H. 0.033 m.; est. rim diam. 0.18 m.

Antithetical spiral (F.M. 50); monochrome
inside.

Light pinkish buff clay; dull black glaze,
worn.

L.H. IIIC.

SUBMYCENAEAN

189. Deep bowl. Pl. 17.

H 451. Rest. H. 0.089 m.

All of rim restored, probably incorrectly, as
too flaring.

Body glazed on outside to just below handle
level; lower body and foot unglazed. Inside and
handles (apparently) glazed.

Brownish buff clay, somewhat pitted; red
to dark brown glaze, badly peeled.

Eleventh century B.C.

PROTOGEOMETRIC

190. Oinochoe. Pl. 17.

H 496. H. 0.227 m.; max. diam. 0.136 m.

Intact but for part of mouth. Band handle
and flaring ring foot. Double vertical dot row
down reserved shoulder in front; to either side,
two sets of compass-drawn concentric semi-
circles (8), centers filled with hourglasses. On
handle, ladder pattern, lowest rung a ring; inside of mouth glazed.

Greatly pitted and flaked pinkish buff clay;
shiny black glaze.

With its proportions this oinochoe is late:
over-pointed oval body, dainty foot, low slim
neck; cf. Desborough, *Protogeometric Pottery*,
pp. 47 ff.

Late Protogeometric.

191. Oinochoe. Pl. 17.

H 254 (NM 16063). H. 0.208 m.; max.
diam. 0.115 m.

Intact but for greater part of band handle.
Four large latticed triangles on neck; ladder
pattern (apparently) on handle.

Black glaze.

Late Protogeometric.

192. Giant skyphoid krater. Pl. 17.

H 487. Rest. H. 0.22 m.; diam. at rim
0.244 m.

Conical base restored. On shoulder lattice
panel and sets of compass-drawn concentric
circles (13). Beside lattice panel, at one side
only, a column of solid lozenges.

Thick shiny black glaze.

A Type IIa skyphoid krater. Desborough,
Protogeometric Pottery, pp. 80, 82-84.

Late Protogeometric.

193. Fragment of a giant skyphoid krater.
Pl. 17.

H 490. P.H. 0.15 m.; diam. at rim 0.212 m.

About half of body preserved. Maltese
crosses with latticed arms within sets of concentric circles. Now lost.

Dull glaze, black to brown.
Type II*b*, cf. Desborough, *Protogeometric Pottery*, pp. 80, 84-85.
Late Protogeometric.

194. Fragment of a giant skyphoid krater.
                                                    Pl. 17.
H 492. P.H. 0.147 m.; est. diam. at rim 0.28 m.
Straight rim, slightly thickened and flaring at its upper edge. Flat upper face of rim reserved and decorated with groups of short vertical strokes. Now lost.
Thick shiny black glaze.
Type IV*b,* cf. Desborough, *Protogeometric Pottery*, pp. 80, 88-89.
Late Protogeometric.

195. Base of a krater.   Pl. 17.
H 597. P.H. 0.09 m.
Dull black glaze.
Other large bases are listed by E. L. Smithson, *Hesperia* 30, 1961, p. 167, under no. 46. The Hymettos base referred to there is the present one, but it is in the Agora Museum, not the National Museum. To the list add *Thorikos* II, p. 32, fig. 20; Δελτ. 28, 1973, Μελ., pls. 15, β, 27, ε.
Late Protogeometric.

196. Kantharos (?).   Pl. 17.
H 615. H. 0.10 m.; est. rim diam. 0.10 m.
Half the body missing. All glazed inside and out except for dot on floor and reserved bands at rim.
Most probably a kantharos like *Kerameikos* IV, pl. 21, inv. no. 2026. The vessel could also be a one-handled cup like *Kerameikos* IV, pl. 24, inv. nos. 1082 and 1104.
Late Protogeometric.

EARLY GEOMETRIC

197. Neck of an amphora.   Pl. 18.
H 465. P.H. 0.146 m.
Glaze band around edge of rim inside; ladder pattern on handle.
Thick brown glaze.

Cf. *Kerameikos* V, 1, pl. 25, inv. no. 253.
E.G. II.

198. Oinochoe.   Pl. 18.
H 457. Rest. H. 0.147 m.; max. diam. 0.105 m.
Mouth and neck restored. Ring foot.
Thick shiny black glaze.
E.G. II–M.G. I.

199. Large one-handled cup.   Pl. 18.
H 445. H. 0.084 m.; diam. at rim 0.15 m.
Complete. Two warts on front, glazed over; inside, reserved dot on floor and band at rim with sets of short strokes. Ladder pattern on band handle.
Shiny black to red glaze.
Other large cups are listed by E. L. Smithson, *Hesperia* 37, 1968, p. 97, note 48. It is best to follow Smithson and not speculate on the possible symbolic meaning of warts on pots. For recent discussion on the subject, see J. Bouzek, *Eirene* 8, 1970, pp. 104-110.
E.G. II.

200. One-handled cup.   Pl. 18.
H 468. H. 0.062 m.; diam. at rim 0.085 m.
Intact. All glazed inside and out except for reserved band on either side of rim; ladder pattern on band handle.
Black glaze.
E.G. II.

201. One-handled cup.   Pl. 18.
H 485. H. 0.059 m.; diam. at rim 0.085 m.
Intact. All glazed inside and out except for reserved dot on floor inside, upper edge of rim; ladder pattern and St. Andrew's cross on handle.
Thick black glaze.
Cf. *Kerameikos* V, 1, pl. 105, inv. nos. 250 and 933.
E.G. II.

MIDDLE GEOMETRIC

202. Oinochoe.   Pl. 18.
H 251 (NM 16112). H. 0.196 m.; max. diam. 0.129 m.

Intact. High ring foot.
Shiny black glaze.
Somewhat later than *Kerameikos* V, 1, pl.
70, inv. no. 2137.
M.G. I.

203. Oinochoe. Pl. 18.

H 356. H. 0.192 m.; max. diam. 0.132 m.
Low ring foot. Ladder pattern and eight-
armed cross on handle.
Black glaze.
Cf. *Kerameikos* V, 1, pl. 73, inv. no. 2145.
M.G. I.

204. Fragment of a skyphos. Pl. 18.

H 611. P.H. 0.06 m.; est. diam. at rim
0.12 m.
Short, flaring rim; rounded shoulder (nothing
of lower body). Glazed inside as far as preserved except for reserved band at rim.
Thick black glaze.
Cf. Πρακτικά, 1939, p. 30, fig. 3, ζ-λ; Δελτ. 28,
1973, Μελ., pl. 29, β, upper left.
M.G. I.

205. Oinochoe. Pl. 18.

H 355. H. 0.217 m.; max. diam. 0.156 m.
Low ring foot. On handle, ladder pattern.
Shiny dark brown glaze.
Cf. *Kerameikos* V, 1, pl. 75, inv. no. 298.
M.G. II.

206. Skyphos. Pl. 18.

H 99 (NM 16086). H. 0.082 m.; diam. at
rim 0.119 m.
Complete. Ring foot. All glazed inside
except for reserved dot on floor and three bands
at rim.
Shiny black glaze.
Cf. *Kerameikos* V, 1, pl. 92, inv. no. 238.
M.G. II.

207. Skyphos. Pl. 18.

H 302. H. 0.068 m.; diam. at rim 0.119 m.
Low disk foot.
Black to reddish brown glaze.
The decorative scheme in the handle zone

appears to be strictly Middle Geometric: cf.
J. N. Coldstream, *Arch. Anz.* 78, 1963, cols.
202-203.
M.G. II.

208. Skyphos. Pl. 18.

H 284. Rest. H. 0.067 m.; diam. at rim
0.123 m.
Nothing of base.
Black glaze.
Like Brann I 35.
M.G. II.

209. Skyphos. Pl. 18.

H 300. H. 0.06 m.; diam. at rim 0.09 m.
Reserved dot at center of floor inside, band
at rim.
Black glaze.
Cf. Brann I 32; also J. N. Coldstream, *Arch.
Anz.* 78, 1963, col. 203.
M.G. II.

210. Skyphos. Pl. 18.

H 299. Rest. H. 0.059 m.; diam. at rim
0.104 m.
Nothing of base.
Black glaze.
M.G. II.

211. Skyphos. Pl. 18.

H 34 (NM 16135). H. 0.064 m.; diam. at
rim 0.101 m.
Shiny black to dull reddish brown glaze.
The gear pattern is rare on Attic skyphoi;
another example, *Ath. Mitt.* 81, 1966, Beil. 14:
4, no. 7.
M.G. II.

212. Skyphos. Pl. 18.

H 295. H. 0.056 m.; diam. at rim 0.098 m.
Low disk foot.
Red glaze.
For the decorative motif in the handle zone,
see Young, *Hesperia*, Suppl. II, 1939, p. 217;
two later examples, *Ath. Mitt.* 88, 1973, pl. 8:
1, no. 3, 2, no. 2.
M.G. II.

213. Skyphos.   Pl. 18.

H. 287. Rest. H. 0.065 m.; diam. at rim 0.11 m.

Bottom completely restored. Compass-drawn rings.

Dark brown glaze.

M.G. II.

214. Skyphos.   Pl. 18.

H 286. Rest. H. 0.067 m.; diam. at rim 0.117 m.

Base completely restored.

Dull black glaze.

Young XX 1-3 and Brann 261 are similarly decorated but deeper and less rounded so probably later than ours. **212** and the two previous skyphoi have less decoration, thus creating a lighter ground in the handle zone; this practice began before the Late Geometric period: cf. Coldstream, *G.G.P.*, pp. 24, 50.

M.G. II.

215. Skyphos.   Pl. 18.

H 285. H. 0.066 m.; diam. at rim 0.104 m.

Dark brown glaze.

M.G. II–L.G. I.

216. Kantharos.   Pl. 19.

H. 430. H. to rim 0.064 m.; diam. at rim 0.09 m.

Flat bottom. Ladder pattern and blob stars on handles.

Dull black glaze, brownish where thin.

Cf. Brann 169.

M.G. II.

217. Kantharos.   Pl. 19.

H 325. H. to rim 0.063 m.; diam. at rim 0.095 m.

Rising band handles applied against shoulder and decorated with ladder pattern.

Shiny black glaze.

M.G. II.

218. Mug.   Pl. 19.

H 26 (NM 16062). H. 0.061 m.; max. diam. 0.07 m.

Flat bottom. Ladder pattern on beginning of handle at top; three glaze bands on rim inside. Black glaze, brown where thin.

Like the mugs from the Isis Grave, *C.V.A.*, Athens 1[1], 4[4], 1-4.

M.G. II.

219. Tankard.   Pl. 19.

H 44 (NM 16167). H. 0.058 m.; max. diam. 0.059 m.

Complete but for handle.

Black glaze.

Other examples: *Ath. Mitt.* 28, 1903, Beil. XXIV, 4; *Hesperia* 19, 1950, pl. 104, b; *Kerameikos* V, 1, pl. 111, inv. no. 831. The tankard developed from the mug in the latter part of the Middle Geometric period: cf. Coldstream, *G.G.P.*, p. 23.

M.G. II.

220. Tankard with double body.   Pl. 19.

H 331. H. 0.061 m.; max. diam. 0.075 m.

Flat bottom and two-storeyed body.

Black glaze shading to red.

M.G. II.

221. Two-handled cup.   Pl. 19.

H 307. H. 0.073 m.; max. diam. 0.094 m.

Unpainted two-handled cups are discussed under Brann 152. Ours is closer to Agora examples which were found in Middle Geometric contexts.

M.G. II.

222. Two-handled cup.   Pl. 19.

H 425. H. 0.082 m.; diam. at rim 0.098 m.

All glazed except for lower edge of foot and a reserved band on either side of rim. On each handle a St. Andrew's cross.

Dull red glaze.

M.G. II.

223. Lid of a pyxis.   Pl. 19.

H 80 (NM 16094). H. with handle 0.026 m.; diam. 0.11 m.

Very slightly convex lid, almost flat; plain

rim, slightly thickened below; large inverted conical handle.

Black glaze.
Cf. Brann I 59.
M.G. II–L.G. I.

224. Large oinochoe.   Pl. 19.

H 357. H. 0.306 m.; max. diam. 0.192 m.
Ring foot; raised ring at junction of body and neck.

Shiny black glaze.
Transition to L.G.

225. Oinochoe.   Pl. 19

H 353. H. 0.223 m.; max. diam. 0.156 m.
Handle missing. Low ring foot.
Shiny black glaze.
Transition to L.G.

226. One-handled cup.   Pl. 23.

H 313. H. 0.06 m.; diam. at rim 0.094 m.
Flat bottom. Glazed inside except for a reserved band at rim.

Dull red to brown glaze outside, thick brown glaze inside.
Like Brann 177.
Transition to L.G.

LATE GEOMETRIC

227. Oinochoe.   Pl. 19.

H 83 (NM 16055). H. 0.238 m.; max. diam. 0.156 m.
Ring foot and rolled handle. In handle zone three narrow glaze lines interrupted in front by a panel filled with a bird with latticed body to right, dot rosettes and latticed triangles in field.
Dull black glaze.
Cf. *Kerameikos* V, 1, pl. 76, inv. no. 274.
L.G. I.

228. Oinochoe.   Pl. 19.

H 85 (NM 16053). H. 0.216 m.; max. diam. 0.151 m.
Ring foot and double rolled handle. Two narrow glaze lines interrupted in front by a zigzag column. Double glaze band down outer face of each handle section.

Shiny brown glaze, in places shading to red.
Cf. Brann 48.
L.G. I.

229. Squat oinochoe.   Pl. 19.

H 250 (NM 16176). H. 0.154 m.; max. diam. 0.111 m.
Ring foot. On handle ladder pattern interrupted by a panel with parallel verticals.
Shiny black glaze.
Probably later than the examples from the Isis Grave, *C.V.A.*, Athens 1[1], 3[3], 8-10, 12, 13.
L.G. I.

230. Squat oinochoe.   Pl. 19.

H 9 (NM 16179). H. 0.12 m.; max. diam. 0.106 m.
Low disk foot. Ladder pattern on handle.
Dull black glaze, fired red in places.
Cf. Brann 76.
L.G. I.

231. Squat oinochoe.   Pl. 19.

H 91 (NM 16075). H. 0.124 m.; max. diam. 0.096 m.
Ring foot; double rolled handle, a column of short diagonals bordered by vertical bands on outer face of each section of handle.
Dull black glaze.
L.G. I.

232. Squat oinochoe.   Pl. 22.

H 346. H. 0.104 m.; max. diam. 0.093 m.
Low ring foot.
Shiny brown glaze.
L.G. I.

233. Trefoil jug.   Pl. 19.

H 93 (NM 16061). H. to rim 0.131 m.; max. diam. 0.114 m.
Disk foot; wide neck. In handle zone a checkerboard; panels with 8-armed crosses on handle.
L.G. I.

234. Skyphos.   Pl. 20.

H 262 (NM 16165). H. 0.066 m.; diam. at rim 0.115 m.

Low ring foot. Inside all glazed but for reserved dot on floor and three reserved bands at rim.

Black glaze, fired red in places.

Shape as *Kerameikos* V, 1, pl. 94, inv. no. 269; pl. 97, inv. no. 327.

L.G. I.

235. Skyphos.   Pl. 20.

H 43 (NM 16089). H. 0.06 m.; diam. at rim 0.103 m.

Black glaze, brownish where thin.

The handle-zone decoration is in the " Parian " manner: cf. Coldstream, *G.G.P.*, p. 180; *Délos* XV, pl. XXXI, 61, 74. The skyphos could be a Cycladic import, although the clay is indistinguishable from Attic.

L.G. I.

236. Skyphos.   Pl. 20.

H 291. H. 0.078 m.

All of one side missing. Plain bottom.

Shiny black glaze.

For other bird skyphoi, cf. E. Brann, *Hesperia* 29, 1960, p. 405, no. 4. Brann would attribute all such skyphoi to one shop.

L.G. I.

237. Skyphos.   Pl. 20.

H 298. Rest. H. 0.072 m.; diam. at rim 0.117 m.

Probably to be restored with a flat bottom instead of a disk foot.

Dull black glaze.

Like *Kerameikos* V, 1, pl. 93, inv. no. 875.

L.G. I.

238. Large skyphos.   Pl. 20.

H 82 (NM 16057). H. 0.141 m.; diam. at rim 0.193 m.

High disk foot. Inside all glazed except for a reserved band at rim filled with a series of short vertical strokes.

Black glaze, brown where thin.

See Brann I 27 for other oversized skyphoi.

L.G. I.

239. Large skyphos.   Pl. 20.

H 428. H. 0.095 m.; diam. at rim 0.162 m.

Shiny black glaze.

L.G. I.

240. High-rimmed bowl.   Pl. 20.

H 127. H. 0.058 m.; diam. at rim 0.074 m.

Intact. Flat bottom and slightly convex lower body. Inside all glazed except for a reserved dot at center of floor and three bands below lip.

Black to brown glaze.

Cf. *Kerameikos* V, 1, pl. 98, inv. no. 2158; a more elaborate example: Brann 319. The shape was invented in the Dipylon Workshop but died out in L.G. IB: cf. Coldstream, *G.G.P.*, pp. 34, 48.

L.G. I.

241. Kantharos.   Pl. 20.

H 86 (NM 16058). H. to rim 0.079 m.

Flat bottom and oval mouth. Front and back, a pair of opposed horses facing center, tethered to each side of a floating tripod-like object; ladder pattern on handles. All glazed inside.

Black glaze, brown where thin.

Scenes with horses and tripods are common in Attic Geometric art: cf. S. Benton, *B.S.A.* 35, 1934-1935, pp. 102ff., nos. 2, 4, 6, 8, 14-17. In all other cases, however, the tripod is resting firmly on the ground line. The shape of our kantharos is like *Bull. Metr. Mus.* 31, 1936, p. 43.

L.G. I.

242. Kantharos.   Pl. 20.

H 94 (NM 16070). H. to rim 0.065 m.

Disk foot and oval mouth. All glazed inside.

Thick black glaze inside, thin and brown outside.

Brann lists other clay-ground kantharoi under I 49 and suggests that the idea may have been inspired by analogous shapes of Middle

Helladic Yellow Minyan pottery which have been found in Late Geometric groups.

L.G. I.

243. Fragment of a kantharos. Pl. 21.

H 598. P.W. 0.102 m.; est. diam. of rim 0.14 m.

Part of rounded shoulder and high straight rim. On shoulder, two opposed horses, a stand or manger between them. Inside glazed as far as preserved except for a reserved band below lip.

Brown glaze, shading to red in places.

For other horse and manger scenes, cf. S. Benton, *B.S.A.* 35, 1934-1935, p. 103, note 11; add *Ath. Mitt.* 88, 1973, pl. 6, no. 7; Δελτ. 28, 1973, Μελ., pl. 1, β-δ.

L.G. I.

244. Jug. Pl. 21.

H 89 (NM 16060). H. to rim 0.111 m.; max. diam. 0.099 m.

Down outer face of handle, three straight vertical bands with wavy verticals between them. Inside unglazed except for two glaze bands below lip.

Black to brown glaze.

L.G. I.

245. Tankard. Pl. 21.

H 333. H. to rim 0.107 m.

Neck divided by triple verticals into panels: on either side of handle, four sets of diminishing triangles with apices meeting at center; at front, a deer to right with head bent back as if reaching for something, perhaps the leaves of a branch. Inside unglazed except for two glaze bands below lip; dot row on upper edge of lip.

Shiny black glaze.

This and the following tankards are difficult to date precisely without context. They probably belong to the end of the L.G. I period or the beginning of L.G. II. Later, the rim begins to overhang the widest diameter: cf. Coldstream, *G.G.P.*, p. 86.

L.G. IB–L.G. IIA.

246. Tankard. Pl. 21.

H 334. Rest. H. to rim 0.085 m.

Nothing of bottom. Neck divided by triple verticals into panels; to each side of handle, vertical zigzag column in narrow panel; then, hatched swastika in square panel; wide panel at front containing two opposed birds with hatched bodies; blob-star ringed by dots between the birds, dot rosettes in field. Two glazed bands below lip inside, interior otherwise unglazed. Ladder pattern on handle.

Black to brown glaze.

The birds resemble those of the Swan Painter, though without the distinctive long necks: cf. Coldstream, *G.G.P.*, pp. 70-71.

L.G. IB–L.G. IIA.

247. Tankard. Pl. 21.

H 434. H. to rim 0.088 m.

Triple verticals divide the neck into five panels; on either side of handle, narrow panels of latticing; then, square panels with long-legged birds facing center, vertical dot rows and dot rosettes in field; at front, a four-spoked wheel, dots between spokes, stroke-fringe around outside. Dot series on upper edge of rim; inside unglazed.

Dull glaze, black to dark brown.

For tankard neck panels with birds and dot rosettes, see Brann L 20. The wheel motif in Greek Geometric art has been much discussed. Recently, J. Bouzek, *Eirene* 8, 1970, pp. 98-101, and J. L. Benson, *Horse, Bird, and Man,* Amherst, Mass., 1970, pp. 67-68, claim the motif from the Mycenaean repertory. More likely, however, is the belief of P. Courbin, *La céramique géométrique de l'Argolide,* Paris, 1966, p. 477, that it is merely an outgrowth of the established Geometric linear repertory. It may have passed into textile art, in which case the fringe may be the result of a purely decorative needlework embellishment. On the wheel motif, see also *Agora* VIII, p. 13, with further references.

L.G. IB–L.G. IIA.

248. Tankard.   Pl. 21.

H 426. H. to rim 0.089 m.

Neck divided into three wide panels by chevron columns bordered by vertical wavy lines; in each panel, a long-legged grazing bird on a horizontal chevron column. Dot series on upper edge of lip, single glaze band below lip inside.

Dull black glaze.

L.G. IB–L.G. IIA.

249. Tankard.   Pl. 21.

H 463. Rest. H. 0.093 m.

Nothing of bottom. On handle, ladder pattern twice interrupted by St. Andrew's crosses. Dot series on upper edge of lip. Two glaze bands below lip inside.

Dark brown glaze.

Recalls a finer example from the Agora, Brann 251.

L.G. IB–L.G. IIA.

250. Fragments of a high-stemmed krater.
    Pl. 21.

H 579 a, b. P.H. of b (fragment with handle) 0.114 m.; est. diam. of rim 0.18 m.

Part of rim, shoulder, and one handle preserved, but nothing of lower body or base. Shoulder rounded directly into high, straight rim. Inside glazed as far as preserved except for a reserved band below lip with groups of short vertical strokes.

Thin brown glaze outside, thick and black inside.

Close to Brann 92; see Coldstream, *G.G.P.*, p. 48 for the shape. The handle, like those of the Agora krater, is the simplest form of horned handle, with muzzle outlined and barred: cf. N. Oakshott, *J.H.S.* 86, 1966, pp. 114-132.

L.G. I.

251. Oinochoe.   Pl. 21.

H 354. H. 0.235 m.; max. diam. 0.161 m.
Low ring foot; rolled handle.
Black glaze.
Cf. Brann 49.
Transition to L.G. II.

252. Oinochoe, Concentric Circle Group.
    Pl. 22.

H 96 (NM 16085). H. 0.158 m.; max. diam. 0.105 m.

Very low ring foot; rolled handle. At either side, five large concentric circles with dot in center; at back, alternating straight and wavy horizontal lines to lower handle attachment; to each side of the handle attachment, bird with solid body facing away; zigzags in field. On front, shoulder to bottom, alternating straight and wavy vertical lines; above this, three bands on the uppermost of which stands a horse to right with two wavy streamers or tethers descending from its mouth; zigzags in field.

Dull black glaze, somewhat worn.

For the group and other examples, cf. Coldstream, *G.G.P.*, pp. 74-76. Ours, with the circles predominating and the front picture panel confined to the shoulder, is early in the series. More examples keep turning up all the time: Δελτ. 22, 1967, Χρον., pl. 81, *a*, upper left; Δελτ. 23, 1968, Χρον., pl. 3, lower right; *Ath. Mitt.* 88, 1973, pl. 6, no. 4.

L.G. IIA.

253. Oinochoe, Corinthianizing.   Pl. 2 .

H 456. H. 0.142 m.; max. diam. 0.118 m.
Flat bottom. Ladder pattern on handle.
Black glaze.
In imitation of the Corinthian Light-on-Da k technique in which white paint was used: cf. Brann N 8.
L.G. II.

254. Oinochoe, Corinthianizing.   Pl. 22.

H 349. H. to lip 0.135 m.; max. d.am. 0.094 m.

Flat bottom; rising band handle decorated on its outer face with an elongated St. Andrew's cross.

Black glaze, fired red in places.

The system of complete banding is Corinthian: cf. Brann 55.

L.G. II.

255. Round-mouthed jug. Pl. 22.

H 103. H. to lip 0.141 m.; max. diam. 0.09 m.
Thin brown glaze.
Like **254** but with round instead of trefoil mouth.
L.G. II.

256. Squat oinochoe. Pl. 22.

H 396. P.H. 0.079 m.; max. diam. 0.063 m.
Nothing of mouth or handle. Low ring foot; conical body.
Shiny black glaze, brown where thin.
For other Late Geometric oinochoai with conical bodies, cf. Brann F 13.
L.G. II.

257. Trefoil jug. Pl. 22.

H 365. H. 0.07 m.; max. diam. 0.072 m.
Shape like **244** but with trefoil mouth instead of round mouth. Entirely glazed inside.
Shiny brown glaze.
L.G. II.

258. Round-mouthed jug. Pl. 22.

H 90 (NM 16059). H. 0.118 m.; max. diam. 0.08 m.
Flat bottom; continuous profile.
Black to brown glaze.
Others include *Kerameikos* V, 1, pl. 139, inv. no. 356; *C.V.A.*, Munich 3[9], 117[399], 7-8; *C.V.A.*, Copenhagen 2[2], 70[71], 6; *Thorikos* IV, p. 88, fig. 69.
L. G. IIB.

259. Round-mouthed jug. Pl. 22.

H 364. P.H. 0.062 m.; max. diam. 0.081 m.
Nothing of neck, mouth, or handle. Squat body with flat bottom. At either side, a set of three concentric circles around a dotted quatrefoil; front and back, same scheme: wavy vertical lines to point of greatest diameter; above this, a zigzag; on shoulder, four latticed triangles with dots between their apices (at back, only two triangles, one on either side of handle attachment).
Dark brown to red glaze.
Close to Brann 358.
L.G. II.

260. Tankard. Pl. 22.

H 435. H. to rim 0.088 m.; max. diam. 0.073 m.
Dot series on upper edge of lip; single glaze band below lip inside.
Black glaze, brown where thin.
L.G. II.

261. Small tankard. Pl. 22.

H 52 (NM 16168). H. 0.056 m.; max. diam. (rim) 0.055 m.
Flat bottom; shallow, convex lower body. High, slightly concave neck decorated with four goats, couchant and regardant.
Thin brown glaze.
For the goats see P. Amandry, *Journ. Near East St.* 24, 1965, pp. 149-160, especially figs. 2, 3. Amandry believes that the pose indicates a galloping goat.
L.G. II.

262. Tankard. Pl. 22.

H 98 (NM 16071). H. 0.08 m.; max. diam. 0.062 m.
Complete. Flat bottom; continuous profile; rising band handle. Top of lip glazed; inside unglazed; ladder pattern on handle interrupted by a St. Andrew's cross.
Dull black to red glaze.
L.G. II.

263. Tankard. Pl. 22.

H 92 (NM 16080). H. 0.094 m.; max. diam. (rim) 0.083 m.
Complete. Flat bottom; straight neck, increasing upward. Dot series on upper edge of lip; two glaze bands below lip inside; on handle, alternating sets of bars and St. Andrew's crosses.
Dull black glaze.
L.G. II.

264. Tankard. Pl. 22.

H 449. H. 0.092 m.; max. diam. of body 0.075 m.
Flat bottom; tall, wide concave neck with flaring rim. Three glaze bands inside at beginning of flare.

Dull glaze, brown to red.
L. G. IIB.

265. Fragmentary tankard, non-Attic.   Pl. 24.

H 497.   H. 0.063 m.

Preserves part of bottom and a third of body and rim. Flat bottom; sharply convex body curving continuously to high, concave neck with flaring rim. On shoulder (presumably at level of handle attachment) a careless lozenge chain; neck divided into panels by sets of five verticals: in narrow panel (one preserved) three short zigzags; in wide panels (two preserved) an animal (goat or deer?) with solid body and outlined head thrown back, at gallop. Series of dots on upper edge of lip; inside unglazed except for two glaze bands below lip.

Pale brown clay with grit; creamy slip with slightly greenish tinge; dull black glaze, badly worn.
L.G. II.

266. Basket-handled jug.   Pl. 22.

H 330.   H. to rim 0.065 m.; max. diam. 0.069 m.

Flat bottom; rolled handle across the mouth. Inside unglazed; three glaze bands on handle.
Thin brown glaze, in places thick and black.
L.G. II.

267. Skyphos.   Pl. 22.

H 296.   H. 0.075 m.; diam. at rim 0.111 m.
Dull red glaze.
Like Brann O 19.
L.G. IIA.

268. Skyphos.   Pl. 22.

H 452.   H. 0.07 m.; diam. at rim 0.107 m.
Thick reddish brown glaze.
Like **267**.
L.G. IIA.

269. Kotyle, Protocorinthianizing.   Pl. 22.

H 433.   H. 0.051 m.; diam. at rim 0.086 m.
Black glaze, fired red in places.
A close parallel to Brann 153, the earliest Corinthianizing kotyle found in the Agora; for its profile, see *Hesperia* 29, 1960, p. 408, fig. 4.
L.G. IIA.

270. Skyphos, metallic imitation.   Pl. 23.

H 420.   H. 0.051 m.; diam. at rim 0.128 m.
Flat bottom; shallow convex body; offset rim, tilted outward. Outside: bands and zigzags. Inside: procession of birds and horses to right (five horses and one bird partially preserved); in field, double zigzag sections, concentric lozenges, vertical wavy lines; center of floor, an 8-armed swastika. Underneath, on resting surface, two glaze rings.
Dull black glaze, much peeled outside.

The shape, which is based on a metallic prototype, is discussed by Young, *Hesperia,* Suppl. II, 1939, pp. 202-203. The latest list of those with figured zones was compiled by B. Schweitzer, *Die geometrische Kunst Griechenlands,* Köln, 1969, p. 324, note 67. The shape was a favorite in the Birdseed Workshop: see the list by Coldstream, *G.G.P.,* p. 68, nos. 20-28, to which may also belong Πρακτικά, 1959, pl. 2, β and Δελτ. 23, 1968, Χρον., pl. 3, upper middle, as well as *Ath. Mitt.* 88, 1973, pl. 5: 1, no. 7 and pl. 7: 2, no. 1. Other figured examples: *Thorikos* IV, p. 81, figs. 55-56 (horses); *Arch. Anz.* 83, 1968, p. 127, figs. 6, 7 (grazing deer); Δελτ. 23, 1968, Χρον., pl. 46, β, middle (lions).

Ours may be from the Workshop of Athens 894: cf. Coldstream, *G.G.P.,* pp. 58-64.
L.G. IIB.

271. Skyphos.   Pl. 23.

H 289.   Rest. H. 0.061 m.; diam. at rim 0.106 m.
Base and lower body all restored.
Shiny brown glaze, peeled.
A step removed from **236**. It could be early or late: Brann L 26 (L.G. IIA); Brann 131 (L.G. IIB).
L.G. II.

272. Skyphos.   Pl. 23.

H 292.   H. 0.04 m.; diam. at rim 0.088 m.
Low disk foot and very squat body. In handle zone, at one side, two birds with striped

bodies to right, a third bird with solid body squeezed in at right; on other side, two opposed birds facing center, one with solid body, the other with hatched body.

Dull black glaze.

L.G. II.

273. Double skyphos.   Pl. 22.

H 304. H. 0.053 m.; diam. at rim 0.092 m.

Three handles restored. All glazed inside except for a reserved dot at center of floor and three bands below rim.

Dull glaze, brown to red.

For other stacked skyphoi, see *C.V.A.*, Heidelberg 3[27], text, p. 46, under no. 5. To the list add a triple skyphos in the Joseph W. Noble Collection: *Proc. Amer. Phil. Soc.* 112, 1968, p. 371, figs. 1, 2. An unpublished triple skyphos from Merenda, much like ours, is on display in the Brauron Museum.

L.G. II.

274. Kantharos.   Pl. 23.

H 326. Rest. H. to rim 0.055 m.; diam. at rim 0.079 m.

Bottom missing. Ladder pattern and St. Andrew's crosses on handles.

Dull glaze, brown to red.

See **236** for degenerate bird metopes.

L.G. II.

275. Kantharos.   Pl. 23.

H 3 (NM 16173). H. 0.065 m.

Flat bottom and oval mouth. Entirely reserved outside except for a large swastika on either side, and dot rows on upper edge of lip, along outer edges of handles, and across bottom of lower handle attachments. All glazed inside except for a reserved dot at center of floor.

Dull black glaze.

See **242** for other clay-ground kantharoi.

L.G. II.

276. Kantharos.   Pl. 23.

H 429. H. to rim 0.062 m.; diam. at rim 0.088 m.

Neither handle preserved. Flat bottom;

squat, rounded body with slightly outward-turned lip. At level of handle zone, elongated blobs surrounded by dots to either side of a zigzag. Completely glazed interior.

Dull black glaze.

Brann 173 has a similar continuous profile.

L.G. II.

277. Kantharos.   Pl. 23.

H 102 (NM 16084). H. to rim 0.064 m.; diam. at rim 0.087 m.

Complete. Disk foot; pointed lower body; high, slightly concave rim. Ladder pattern on handles. Inside all glazed except for a reserved dot at center of floor and three reserved bands at rim.

Dull black glaze, brownish where thin.

For the shape, cf. Brann 175.

L.G. IIB.

278. Kantharos.   Pl. 23.

H 88 (NM 16088). H. 0.064 m.

Flat bottom and oval mouth. Inside all glazed except for a reserved band at rim.

Shiny red glaze.

The simple outlined cross is a common Argive Geometric motif but is rare in Attic Geometric.

L.G. IIB.

279. Kantharos.   Pl. 23.

H 442. H. to rim 0.055 m.

Flat bottom and oval mouth. All glazed inside.

Shiny red glaze.

Shape like *Kerameikos* V, 1, pl. 88, inv. nos. 320, 323, 324.

L.G. IIB.

280. One-handled cup.   Pl. 23.

H 314. H. 0.07 m.; diam. at rim 0.095 m.

Flat bottom. All glazed inside and out except for two reserved bands on rim outside and one inside, and dot on floor.

Thick, shiny red glaze.

L.G. IIB.

281. Phaleron cup.   Pl. 23.

H 317. H. 0.056 m.; diam. at rim 0.09 m.
Slightly convex side wall.
Shiny black to reddish brown glaze.
Cf. Brann 190.
L. G. IIB.

282. Phaleron cup.   Pl. 23.

H 466. H. 0.05 m.; diam. at rim 0.091 m.
Ladder pattern on handle; all glazed inside
except for a reserved band halfway up body
and another at rim.
Dull black to brown glaze.
The common flaring calyx variety, as Brann
193.
L. G. IIB.

283. Phaleron cup.   Pl. 24.

H 40 (NM 16098). H. 0.44 m.; diam. at
rim 0.08 m.

Intact but for handle. All glazed inside
except for a reserved band just below the lip.
Cf. *Kerameikos* V, 1, pl. 107, inv. no. 352;
Δελτ. 28, 1973, Μελ., pl. 24, στ.
L.G. IIB.

284. Phaleron cup.   Pl. 23.

H 310. H. 0.05 m.; diam. at rim 0.075 m.
All glazed inside.

Dull black glaze, shading in places to red.
Cf. *Thorikos* IV, p. 78, fig. 49.
L.G. IIB.

285. Trefoil cup.   Pl. 24.

H 422. H. 0.066 m.
Flat bottom; flaring rim pinched to trefoil
mouth. Elongated sigmas on outside; row of
dots on outer face of lip. Lip reserved inside
and decorated with elongated dots linked by
tangents; otherwise glazed inside except for a
reserved dot on the floor. Ladder pattern and
St. Andrew's cross on handle.
Shiny black glaze.
For other trefoil cups, see Brann O 32; add
to the list *C.V.A.*, Geneva 1[1], 5[5], 5; Δελτ.

18, 1963, Χρον., pl. 41, γ; *Ath. Mitt.* 88, 1973,
pl. 8: 2, no. 4.
L.G. IIB.

286. Trefoil cup.   Pl. 24.

H 17 (NM 16078). H. 0.069 m.
Like **285**.
L.G. IIB.

287. Cup with disparate handles.   Pl. 24.

H 437. H. 0.04 m.; diam. at rim 0.078 m.
Flat bottom; high, flaring upper wall; one
vertical band handle (missing but restored
correctly as indicated by handle attachments),
and one horizontal rolled handle. Inside all
glazed except for a reserved band just below lip.
Dull glaze, black to red.
Others: *C.V.A.*, Cambridge 1[6], 1[239],
16; Δελτ. 28, 1973, Μελ., pl. 10, α, β (with
lids); unpublished examples include one from
Merenda on display in the Brauron Museum
and another from Eleusis in the Eleusis Museum.
L.G. II.

288. Rim sherd of a cup.   Pl. 24.

H 591. P.H. 0.05 m.
Straight wall; plain lip. From left to right:
man with sword (head missing), a shield-like
object, and a bird(?) facing right. Glazed
inside as far as preserved except for a reserved
band below the lip.
Shiny black glaze.
L.G. II.

289. Rim fragment of a cup or skyphos.
                                          Pl. 21.

H 593. P.H. 0.041 m.; est. diam. of rim
0.09 m.
Slightly rounded shoulder continuous with
plain lip. Outside reserved and decorated with
a man leading a horse with spike mane to right,
zigzags in field. Glazed inside as far as preserved.
Dull glaze, black to red.
Perhaps by a follower of the artists in the

Sub-Dipylon Group: cf. Coldstream, *G.G.P.,* pp. 55-56.

L.G. II.

290. Rim fragment of a round-mouthed jug. Pl. 24.

H 594. P.H. 0.051 m.

Preserves part of high, vertical neck and flaring round mouth. Neck reserved and decorated with a row of pointed-handled tripod-cauldrons. Inside unglazed as far as preserved, except for three glaze bands at rim.

For depictions of tripod-cauldrons on Geometric vases, see S. Benton, *B.S.A.* 35, 1934-1935, pp. 102-108. None of those listed is like the tripods on our fragment, with streamer-like wavy lines between the legs; for tripods quite like ours, see *C.V.A.,* Reading 1[12], 8[535], 5.

L.G. II.

291. Rim fragment of a kantharos(?). Pl. 24.

H 599. P.H. 0.04 m.

Shoulder rounded directly into plain rim. On outside, shield and bird (apparently). Inside glazed as far as preserved.

Brown glaze.

Probably like *Kerameikos* V, 1, pl. 88, inv. nos. 323, 324; a similar shield, *Ath. Mitt.* 88, 1973, pl. 10, no. 2.

L.G. IIB.

SUBGEOMETRIC AND PROTOATTIC

292. Subgeometric skyphos. Pl. 24.

H 440. H. 0.071 m.; diam. at rim 0.11 m.

Entirely glazed inside and out except for a reserved band on either side of rim; the band inside decorated with a stroke series.

Dull glaze, black to dark brown and somewhat peeled.

Cf. Brann 137.

Late eighth century B.C.

293. Fragmentary squat jug, Subgeometric. Pl. 24.

H 498. H. 0.069 m.

Large portion of the body at one side, handle, and most of neck and mouth missing. Ring foot; well-rounded body curving continuously into short, straight neck; flaring trefoil mouth (apparently). Bands and a careless double-lozenge chain on lower body; upper body reserved and decorated, left to right: striding lion to left, mouth open and one leg extended straight out; man to left, his arms outstretched (both hands missing); the man is standing on the tail of an animal (deer or horse?) with long tail (neck and head missing); groups of short wavy lines in field. Two glaze bands on inside of neck, otherwise unglazed inside.

Dull glaze, brown where thick, red where thin.

For lions, see *Agora* VIII, pp. 18-19. The man may be dancing and snapping his fingers: cf. Brann 309.

Ca. 700 B.C.

294. Fragment of a closed vessel, amphora(?). Pl. 26.

H 592. P.H. 0.043 m.

Long, bare legs of two figures to right; hooked and dotted vertical lozenge chain between them. Unglazed inside as far as preserved.

Dark brown glaze.

Early Protoattic.

295. Fragment of an oinochoe. Pl. 24.

H 390. P.H. 0.068 m.

Nothing of handle or mouth. Flat bottom; squat, convex lower body; high, upward-tapering upper wall. Legs and round shield of a man walking right and carrying two spears (head missing); behind, tree (?) with spiral-like leaves.

Black glaze, brown where thin.

Cf. Brann E 1 for depiction of round shields with devices. The shape is probably akin to Brann F 13.

Early Protoattic.

296. Small oinochoe, Subgeometric. Pl. 25.

H 120. P.H. 0.077 m.; max. diam. 0.072 m.

Handle and most of trefoil mouth restored. Disk foot, sharply offset from body.

Streaky brown glaze, much worn and peeled.
Cf. Brann 58.
Early seventh century B.C.

297. Jug aryballos, Subgeometric.   Pl. 25.

H 342. H. 0.087 m.; max. diam. 0.082 m.
Flat bottom and round mouth. Irregular latticing on shoulder, probably first of triangles, then spaces between.
Dull red glaze.
Cf. Brann 65.
Early seventh century B.C.

298. Kotyle, Protocorinthianizing.   Pl. 24.

H 87 (NM 16095). H. 0.116 m.; diam. at rim 0.145 m.
Disk foot; fairly pointed body. All glazed inside except for two reserved bands below lip, the upper decorated with groups of short strokes.
Black to brown glaze.
For the Corinthian model of this type of kotyle, see Brann 155. Ours dates just before the beginning of a tenser profile and appearance of base rays.
Early seventh century B.C.

299. Kotyle, Protocorinthianizing.   Pl. 25.

H 397. H. 0.097 m.; diam. at rim 0.111 m.
Red glaze.
Cf. Brann 159; *Kerameikos* V, 1, pl. 132, neg. no. 5541.
Early seventh century B.C.

300. Kotyle, Protocorinthianizing.   Pl. 24.

H 459. H. 0.053 m.
Handle and most of body at one side restored. Warts in place of other handle.
Thin streaky black glaze.
Cf. *A.J.A.* 46, 1942, p. 29, fig. 6: 27.4.
Early seventh century B.C.

301. Skyphos, metallic imitation.   Pl. 23.

H 439. H. 0.043 m.; diam. at rim 0.10 m.
Flat bottom; wide, shallow body; offset rim, tilted outward. Body banded to handle zone;

in handle zone, a zigzag; parallel verticals on either side of rim; banded inside.
Black glaze outside, mostly peeled; dull reddish brown glaze inside.
Cf. Brann L 28.
Early seventh century B.C.

302. Skyphos, Subgeometric.   Pl. 24.

H 288. H. 0.060 m.; diam. at rim 0.107 m.
Entirely glazed inside and out except for the reserved handle zone outside.
Streaky black glaze.
Cf. Brann 139.
First half of seventh century B.C.

303. Two-handled cup, Subgeometric. Pl. 25.

H 421. Rest. H. 0.072 m.; diam. at rim 0.115 m.
All of base and both handles restored; perhaps a more pointed lower body than restored. Inside all glazed except for three reserved bands below lip, the uppermost of which is decorated with groups of short strokes.
Dull reddish brown glaze.
Cf. Young XII 7, a deep two-handled variety of the cup on stand.
First half of seventh century B.C.

304. One-handled cup with lid.   Pl. 25.

H 392. H. to rim 0.05 m.; diam. at rim 0.065 m.
Low ring foot; shallow, concave lid with spike knob handle. Cup: on lower body, dots in parentheses separated by verticals; in handle zone, diagonal columns and a panel with some kind of hooked ornament (the rest of the zone is missing); on rim, running-dog pattern with dots between; inside all glazed except for two reserved bands on rim. Lid: row of dots on outer edge; then, bands and running-dog pattern with dots between; on handle, bands and a zone of latticed lozenges; unglazed underneath.
Shiny red glaze.
Early Protoattic.

305. One-handled cup(?), Subgeometric.
Pl. 25.

H 398. H. 0.07 m.; diam. at rim 0.076 m.

Handle and most of the body at the other side missing and restored. In handle zone, a panel containing a double zigzag with arced lines at either end; all glazed inside except for two reserved bands on rim.

Probably to be restored as a kantharos: cf. *Kerameikos* V, 1, pl. 88, inv. no. 1229.

Early seventh century B.C.

306. Fragmentary lamp.
Pl. 25.

H 573. Max. dim. 0.082 m.

Broken away just before the handle attachment behind and at beginning of nozzle in front.

Gritty, micaceous clay, pinkish buff at core, grayish brown at surface; unglazed. Handmade.

A cocked-hat lamp, Type I; cf. *Agora* IV, pp. 7-8.

First half of seventh century B.C.

307. Oinochoe, Protoattic.
Pl. 25.

H 391. P.H. 0.082 m.; max. diam. 0.057 m.

Nothing of handle or mouth. Low ring foot; continuous profile.

Dull glaze, black to brown.

Cf. *A.J.A.* 46, 1942, p. 50, for a discussion of the type.

Mid-seventh century B.C.

308. Plate, Subgeometric.
Pl. 25.

H 419. H. 0.04 m.; diam. at rim 0.17 m.

Disk foot; slightly convex side wall; plain rim, thickened inward and flat on top. Stroke series on top of rim; all glazed inside.

Dull glaze, black to brown.

Cf. Brann F 29.

Third quarter of seventh century B.C.

309. Fragmentary lamp.
Pl. 26.

H 574 a, b. Max. dim. of b (larger fragment) 0.062 m.

Two non-joining fragments of the same lamp, preserving the back (a) and most of one side (b); nozzle and handle broken away. Vertical band handle at back as indicated by attachments, from just above base to edge of rim.

Brownish buff clay with grit; streaky dull brown glaze, inside only. Wheelmade.

A cocked-hat lamp, Type 3; cf. *Agora* IV, p. 12.

Fourth quarter of seventh century B.C.

310. Bowl, Subgeometric.
Pl. 25.

H 399. H. 0.049 m.; diam. at rim 0.138 m.

Flat bottom; thickened rim, projecting slightly outward and flat on top. Banded outside; stroke series on top of rim; all glazed inside.

Dull red glaze.

Seventh century B.C.

311. Kalathos, Protogeometricizing.
Pl. 26.

H 587. H. 0.046 m.; diam. at bottom 0.04 m.

Complete profile preserved: flat bottom, cylindrical body, wide flaring rim. Inside completely glazed except for three reserved bands at rim, and floor which is reserved and decorated with a glaze dot.

Shiny black glaze.

Seventh century B.C.

312. Trefoil jug, cooking ware.
Pl. 26.

H 360. Rest. H. 0.081 m.; max. diam. 0.091 m.

Bottom wholly restored. Incised wavy lines at level of both handle attachments and down outer face of handle.

Unglazed and handmade.

See E. Brann, *Hesperia* 30, 1961, pp. 316-317, for a discussion of this ware; for incised decoration on cooking ware, see Brann 612-617. The fabric and technique of modeling were refined in the sixth century: cf. *Agora* XII, pp. 34-36. No cooking-ware jugs of comparably small size are reported from the Agora or Kerameikos, but see jugs like ours from Anavyssos: Πρακτικά, 1911, p. 124, especially nos. 25, 27.

Seventh century B.C.

313. Terracotta horse figurine.   Pl. 26.

H 157. H. to head 0.065 m.

Three of the legs restored. Mane pinched to a sharp, straight ridge; tail applied against left rear leg. Faint traces of glaze show that the horse was glazed over most of its body, with reserved bands on neck and over mane.

Pinkish buff clay with grit; dull red glaze, almost completely worn away.

Cf. Young, *Hesperia*, Suppl. II, 1939, pp. 224-225, for Subgeometric horses.

Seventh century B.C.

314. Fragmentary aryballos, Corinthian.

Pl. 26.

H 374. P.H. 0.051 m.

Nothing of neck, mouth, or handle.

Light greenish buff clay, Corinthian; black to brown glaze.

Cf. *Corinth* XIII, pl. 12, Grave 65-1 with ray base; *Perachora* II, pl. 2, nos. 35, 37.

Middle Protocorinthian–Late Protocorinthian.

315. Fragment of an alabastron, Corinthian.

Pl. 26.

H 560. P.H. 0.063 m.

A fragment from the side wall, mended from two pieces. Part of a lion with elaborately incised mane; over back of lion, a large incised rosette. Unglazed inside as far as preserved.

Greenish buff Corinthian clay; dull black glaze.

Cf. H. Payne, *Necrocorinthia*, Oxford, 1931, pl. 15: 7, 8.

Similar (fragments from same shape): H 558 (with part of a bird or siren), H 559 (with part of a bird).

Late Transitional.

316. Fragment of a closed vessel, Corinthian.
Pl. 26.

H 561. Max. dim. 0.021 m.

Probably from the wall of an alabastron. Part of a winged figure running right: part of torso with wing, extended left arm, and knee;

figure is wearing an incised short-sleeved chiton.

Cf. H. Payne, *Necrocorinthia*, pl. 15: 10 for a similar chiton.

Late Transitional.

317. Votive oinochoe, Argive monochrome.

Pl. 26.

H 377. H. 0.062 m.

Stroke polishing on neck. Unglazed and handmade.

Small, unpainted votives are found in great quantities at many sanctuary sites. Only about 100 were saved from the dump on Hymettos, although the total number found was probably much greater. Most of those saved resemble examples from the Athenian Agora published by Young, *Hesperia*, Suppl. II, 1939, p. 157, fig. 111, C 71-C 76. Dates can be assigned to these small votives only when they are found in datable contexts. They seem to occur with equal frequency throughout the 8th and 7th centuries B.C. For the fabric and dating, see P. Courbin, *La céramique géométrique de l'Argolide*, pp. 29 ff., 70 ff.

Eighth–seventh century B.C.

318. Votive two-handled cup, Argive   Pl. 26.
monochrome.

H 207. H. 0.05 m.

Both handles restored. Low irregular base with wheel marks on the bottom. Unglazed.

Eighth–seventh century B.C.

319. Votive one-handled cup.   Pl. 26.

H 108. H. 0.024 m.

Wheelmade. Dull black glaze all over.

Eighth–seventh century B.C.

320. Iron spatula.   Pl. 26.

H 581. L. 0.136 m.; Th. 0.003 m.

Intact, but surface badly corroded and end of peen chipped. Thin, flat blade with tapering shaft.

Cf. C. Waldstein, *The Argive Heraeum* II, Boston and New York, 1905, pl. CXXVI, no. 2264.

This and the following metal objects from the dump are assigned to the 7th century B.C., although we cannot be certain of their dating without context. Some of the objects may belong to the 8th or 6th century B.C.

Seventh century B.C.?

321. Iron knife. Pl. 26.

H 582. L. 0.183 m.

Intact. Blunt-ended haft beveled to a chisel edge.

Seventh century B.C.?

322. Iron spit. Pl. 26.

H 580. P.L. 0.173 m.

Broken off at one end. Preserved end hammered flat into form of a pointed oval. Two others uninventoried.

Recent discussion on iron spits: Coldstream, *G.G.P.*, pp. 362-363; M. Oeconomides, *A.A.A.* 2, 1969, pp. 442-445.

Seventh century B.C.?

323. Iron needle. Pl. 26.

H 586. L. 0.075 m.

Broken off at one end. Round, tapering shaft. One end flattened and a small hole neatly drilled through it. Two others uninventoried.

Seventh century B.C.?

324. Fragmentary bronze chisel. Pl. 26.

H 583. P.L. 0.06 m.

Broken shaft. Shaft flares at preserved end and has a beveled chisel edge.

Seventh century B.C.?

325. Bronze finger ring.

H 584. Diam. 0.023 m.; W. of band 0.005 m.

Intact. Flat band flattened at one side to receive bezel; a narrow hole neatly drilled through band at one side of flattened part. A sunken groove down middle of band with a row of raised dots.

Seventh century B.C.?

SIXTH–SECOND CENTURIES B.C.

326. Kotyle, imitation of Corinthian. Pl. 27.

H 111. H. 0.044 m.; diam. at rim 0.065 m.

Complete. Flaring ring foot; plain rim, slightly inturned; tiny, elongated rolled handles. Dot row in handle zone bordered above and below by single purple bands. All glazed inside. Streaky black glaze.

For a Corinthian example, see *Corinth* XIII, pl. 25, Deposit 43-a; another Attic copy, *Agora* XII, pl. 14, no. 307.

First half of sixth century B.C.

327. Skyphos, Subgeometric survival. Pl. 27.

H 432. H. 0.054 m.; diam. at rim 0.095 m.

Both handles restored. Flat bottom; rim thickened inward and flat on top. All glazed inside and out except for handle zone outside and top of rim decorated with a series of large dots.

Good, lustrous black glaze.

For a discussion of this Subgeometric survival, see *Agora* XII, p. 87.

Mid-sixth century B.C.

328. Small skyphos. Pl. 27.

H 393. Rest. H. 0.046 m.

Both handles and all of lip restored. High, flaring ring foot; pointed body. Foot glazed; rays above; on body, careless blobby palmettes separated by petals; dots along lower edge of rim. Inside all glazed.

Black to brown glaze, badly peeled.

Cf. Πρακτικά, 1934, p. 34, fig. 7.

Sixth century B.C.

329. Base fragment of a Corinthian-type skyphos. Pl. 27.

H 609. Diam. at foot 0.06 m.

Half of foot and lower portion of side wall preserved. Reserved band on wall just above foot painted red; otherwise all glazed inside and out as far as preserved.

Black glaze.

For the type, see *Agora* XII, pp. 81-82.
Sixth century B.C.

330. Type C cup, concave lip.   Pl. 27.

H 616. Max. P. dim. 0.043 m.; est. rim diam.
0.18 m.

A fragment preserving part of the rim and
upper body with one handle attachment.

Good, lustrous black glaze inside and out as
far as preserved.

Like *Agora* XII, pl. 19, nos. 398-400.

Last quarter of sixth century B.C.

331. Saltcellar.   Pl. 27.

H 596. H. 0.026 m.; diam. at rim 0.063 m.

Half preserved. Flat bottom; side wall
slightly incurving at rim; hemispherical bowl
inside. All glazed except for the reserved
resting surface.

Good, lustrous black glaze.

Cf. *Agora* XII, pl. 34, no. 895.

Late fifth century B.C.

332. Fragment of a bronze handle.   Pl. 27.

H 585. Max. dim. 0.055 m.

One end broken off; existing piece bent out
of original shape. Thin, angular band; preserved end a tapering knob with fillet above;
end was purposely bent to form a hook for
affixing to a vessel.

Cf. D. M. Robinson, *Excavations at Olynthus,*
X, *Metal and Minor Miscellaneous Finds,*
Baltimore, 1941, pp. 207-221, pl. LVIII, nos.
737, 746.

First half of fourth century B.C.

333. Fragment of a saucer.   Pl. 27.

H 610. Est. diam. at rim 0.15 m.

Small ring foot; horizontal rim with two
small furrows. All glazed inside and out except
for top of rim which is reserved.

Worn black glaze.

Cf. H. A. Thompson, *Hesperia* 3, 1934, p.
435, for this type of saucer.

Late fourth century B.C.

334. Coin of Athens, AE.   Pl. 27.
H 578.

Obv.: Corinthian-helmeted Athena, r.(?).
Rev.: Owl, r.

Both sides very pitted and practically
illegible.

Cf. J. N. Svoronos, *Les monnaies d'Athènes,*
Munich, 1923-1926, pl. 22, nos. 64-84.

First half of third century B.C.

335. Stamped amphora handle, Knidian.
    Pl. 27.

H 436. P.L. 0.089 m.

Part of neck around handle preserved.

['Ἐπὶ] 'Αριστομή-
[δ]ευς Κνίδων
'Αγα- prow? —θίγ[ου]

A KT 10 stamp (cf. V. Grace and M. Sav-
vatianou-Petropoulakou, *Exploration archéologique de Délos* XXVII, *L'îlot de la Maison
des Comédiens,* Paris, 1970, p. 323), unpublished parallels for which exist on Delos, and
in the Athenian Agora and Kerameikos. Miss
Grace informs me that the stamp probably
belongs to the early part of a period of 20–30
years during which pairs of magistrates were
named on Knidian jars (another on the other
handle in this case).

First quarter of first century B.C.

ROMAN PERIOD

336. Coin of Athens, AE.   Pl. 27.
H 577.

Obv.: Helmeted head of Athena, r.; border
of dots.

Rev.: ΘE; Athena advancing r., armed with
spear and aegis; in front, an owl; the whole in
a wreath of olives.

Very worn both sides; details partially
illegible.

Cf. J. N. Svoronos, *Les monnaies d'Athènes,*
pl. 80, nos. 29-32. J. H. Kroll informs me that
this type of coin occurs in late post-Sullan
hoards of Athens and not before: cf. A. R.

Bellinger, *Amer. Num. Soc. N. Mon.* 42, 1930, p. 11, I.

Augustan period.

337. Base fragment of a lamp, Alpha Globule. Pl. 27.

H 570. Max. dim. 0.033 m.

Part of base and side wall preserved. An alpha in relief, with raised ring; uneven row of globules around body (three rows preserved). Cf. *Agora* VII, pp. 15-16.

Latter part of second century after Christ.

338. Coin of Constantius, AE. Pl. 28.

H 575.

Obv: FL VAL CONSTANTIUS NOB CAES; radiate, draped bust, l.

Rev.: CONCORDIA MILITUM; prince standing r., holding scepter or paragonium, receiving Victory globe from Jupiter, who stands l., holding a scepter. Mint mark: KB.

Cf. C. H. V. Sutherland, *The Roman Imperial Coinage* VI, London, 1967, pl. 14, no. 15a.

Ca. A.D. 295.

339. Lamp. Pl. 28.

H 370. P.L. 0.08 m.

Roof-tile fabric, light brownish buff in color and full of red and brown inclusions.

Disk: bull with filleted horns to left, and two framing rings; paneled rim: 8-S pattern. Bottom, within circle:

EYT–
YXH

Cf. Perlzweig 912; for the signature, *Agora* VII, pp. 34-37, a prolific workshop of the late 3rd–early 4th century after Christ. Mrs. Perlzweig-Binder informs me, however, that the present lamp is from a second-generation mold.

Fourth century after Christ.

340. Lamp. Pl. 28.

H 202. L. 0.09 m.

Disk: rosette and framing band; rim: wavy line. Bottom: incised branch within double almond-shaped groove.

Cf. Perlzweig 1833.

Second half of fourth century after Christ.

341. Coin of Arcadius or Honorius, AE. Pl. 28.

H 576.

Obv.: – – – US PF AUG; draped and filleted bust, r.

Rev.: [VIRTUS] EXER [CITI]; emperor facing, head r., in r. hand a spear, l. hand rests on shield. Victory to l. crowns him with wreath. No mint mark preserved.

Cf. R. G. Carson, P. V. Hill, J. Kent, *Late Roman Bronze Coinage,* A.D. *324-498,* London, 1960, p. 90, nos. 2205-2206.

A.D. 395-408.

342. Fragment of a lamp. Pl. 28.

H 563. P.L. 0.068 m.

Part of disk and rim preserved. Disk: cross monogram with closed rho turned left; circles at center of cross and at end of each arm; rim: concentric half circles.

Cf. Perlzweig 1144.

Late fourth–early fifth century after Christ.

343. Fragment of a multi-nozzle lamp. Pl. 28.

H 572. Max. dim. 0.103 m.

A large fragment from the disk and rim; handle and nozzles all broken away. Disk plain; rim: hatched band and groups of small dotted circles. Burning at points where nozzles are broken away from rim.

Cf. Perlzweig 2020.

Late fourth–early fifth century after Christ.

344. Lamp. Pl. 28.

H 201. L. 0.096 m. *A.J.A.* 44, 1940, p. 4, fig. 6, right.

Intact. Plain disk; rim: herringbone. Bottom: ⊂ᵂ and an inverted, incised branch.

Cf. Perlzweig 2718; for the signature, *Agora* VII, pp. 52-53.

First half of fifth century after Christ.

345. Lamp. Pl. 28.

H 369. L. 0.096 m.

Intact. Disk: crouching lion right and

framing ring; rim: leaves alternating with small globular clusters. Bottom: inverted, incised branch within two almond-shaped grooves.

Cf. Perlzweig 2412.

First half of fifth century after Christ.

346. Lamp.   Pl. 28.

H 204. P.L. 0.081 m.

Disk plain; rim: tendril. Bottom: a kappa turned left, and two rings.

Cf. Perlzweig 2664.

First half of fifth century after Christ.

347. Fragment of a lamp.

H 205. P.L. 0.07 m. *A.J.A.* 44, 1940, p. 4, fig. 6, left.

Nothing of sides or bottom. Disk: long-beaked bird and a rearing animal (wolf?) facing each other across filling hole; rim: leaved tendril.

R. S. Young has suggested that the scene on the disk is from one of Aesop's fables: *A.J.A.* 44, 1940, p. 5.

Cf. O. Broneer, *Corinth*, IV, ii, *Terracotta Lamps*, Cambridge, Mass., 1930, p. 268, no. 1300.

Fifth century after Christ.

348. Lamp.   Pl. 28.

H 375. P.L. 0.084 m.

Bottom all chipped away. Disk plain; rim: relief rings.

Cf. Perlzweig 2854.

Sixth century after Christ.

349. Fragment of a lamp.   Pl. 28.

H 571. Max. dim. 0.038 m.

Part of a disk and rim preserved. Disk: star of David within framing ring; rim: raised pairs of dots.

Cf. Perlzweig 2440.

Sixth century after Christ.

CHRONOLOGY OF THE SANCTUARY

The most remarkable feature of the material is its wide chronological spread, from the Early Bronze Age to the Late Roman period. The actual number of finds is remarkably small, considering the long period of time separating the earliest and latest material, but there are concentrations in certain periods significant enough to suggest when the sanctuary was in regular use. Table 1 gives a breakdown of the pottery by periods, including large numbers of fragmentary vessels which duplicate examples included in the catalogue.

BRONZE AGE. Material dating from the Early, Middle, and Late Helladic periods was found, but the total amount for any given phase is so small as to make it doubtful that any of it had a connection with the later sanctuary. Table 2 gives the total number of prehistoric sherds and vessels from the excavations.

PROTOGEOMETRIC PERIOD. After the latest Bronze Age pottery, a stray Submycenaean goblet is the only piece until Late Protogeometric. No Early or Middle Protogeometric pottery was found. But a number of vessels all belonging to the latest phase of the Protogeometric period indicates that the sanctuary was established at that time, the latter half of the 10th century B.C.

GEOMETRIC PERIOD. Except for E.G. I every phase of the Geometric period is represented by some pottery, with the most occurring in M.G. II and L.G. I–II. The small quantity from E.G. and M.G. I may indicate a decline in activity

	TOTAL	CLOSED SHAPES				OPEN SHAPES							
		Oinochoai and Jugs	Amphoras	Pyxides	Indeterminate	Kraters	One-handled Cups	Stemmed Cups	Kantharoi	Skyphoi	Kotylai	Tankards	Indeterminate
Protogeometric	69	27				34			8				
E.G. II	13	2	1				10						
M.G. I	12	8								4			
M.G. II	91	11		2			10		2	61		5	
L.G. I	82	32				1			3	37		9	
L.G. II	294	35					136		10	39		62	12
7th Century	589	12					180			41	343		13
6th Century	109				7			9		37			56

TABLE 1

		TOTAL	Linear and Monochrome	Patterned	Unpainted
Early Helladic		1			
Middle Helladic		2			
Late Helladic:	Rims	17	10	4	3
	Bases and Stems	8	5	1	2
	Handles	11	6		5
	Body sherds	40	21	12	7

TABLE 2

from Protogeometric, or it may reflect a bias in the sorting of the material. If, for example, the most commonly dedicated vessels in the early phases of the Geometric period were simple, glazed one-handled cups, they might not have attracted the attention of the excavators, and numbers of fragments could have been discarded. Conversely, all of the identifiable Protogeometric pieces were no doubt kept. We should, therefore, avoid concluding that worship at the sanctuary abruptly declined just after Protogeometric.

SEVENTH CENTURY B.C. Activity at the sanctuary was now greater than during any other period, lasting through the entire century.

SIXTH CENTURY B.C. The number of finds is down considerably from the preceding century. The last inscribed dedications and regular offerings were made at this time.

FIFTH–FIRST CENTURIES B.C. The handful of sherds and other objects of these centuries does not constitute much evidence for worship at the sanctuary but does represent sporadic offerings.

ROMAN PERIOD. Some material was deposited at the site mainly in the Late Roman period. Fragments of about 120 lamps indicate some sort of activity in the late 4th and early 5th centuries after Christ. What the nature of that activity was and what connection, if any, it had with the old shrine of Zeus will be investigated in the following chapter.

RITUAL AT THE SANCTUARY

There may have been special days for organized worship services, and a resident priest of Zeus at the sanctuary, although we have no firm evidence for this. Also, it is quite likely that individuals visited the sanctuary whenever they wished, in order to make offerings for rain. The ritual which they followed is not difficult to imagine. An individual would place his offering at the altar to the accompaniment of appropriate prayers, then leave. The next person to come with an offering would brush the previous worshipper's gift unceremoniously to the ground and place his own at the altar. As was often the case in Greek sanctuaries where small, cheap dedicatory gifts were concerned, a particular offering had meaning only to the individual who dedicated it. The next votary did not treat any previous offering with respect but cast it aside without hesitation so that his own gift might receive all the attention. In this way the area around the altar gradually became littered with broken pots, and periodic sweepings of the enclosure were necessary.[5] The old votives were gathered up and thrown into the depression.

[5] For a similar situation at the temple of Hera Limenia at Perachora, see H. Payne, *Perachora* I, Oxford, 1940, pp. 116-117.

As abundant evidence from the votive dump indicates, another feature of the ritual was the sacrificial burning of animal offerings. Although none of the material was kept, the field notebooks mention that many burned animal bones and a considerable amount of ash was found along with the mass of pottery in the depression. But whether it was normal practice for individual worshippers to make animal sacrifices or not is uncertain. Perhaps a sacrifice was made only at certain times, such as during a period of drought or on a special festival day. Whatever the case, as very little of the pottery shows signs of burning, the animal sacrifices were probably made elsewhere than in the altar enclosure where the dedicatory pottery accumulated.

SIGNIFICANCE OF THE OFFERINGS

Enough pottery was recovered to allow for some observations to be made concerning the nature of offerings given to Zeus. The Geometric and Subgeometric pottery is for the most part mediocre. It is simple ware, quite inferior to the magnificent pottery from such cemeteries as those at the Dipylon Gate, Anargyros, and Anavyssos. The Hymettos pottery is instead on a par with the pottery of the same periods from wells in the Athenian Agora and from the Kerameikos cemetery south of the Eridanos. It must represent the ordinary-use pottery of the dedicators' own homes. There are no indications that any of the painted pottery was mass produced for dedication at the altar.

Open shapes preponderate. Especially popular are normal-sized pouring and drinking vessels: oinochoai, jugs, tankards, and two- and one-handled cups.[6] Pyxides, which are standard grave furniture, are naturally almost totally absent. Also poorly represented are amphorae, kraters, and plates. Thus, the predominance of small, ordinary shapes, along with the scarcity of larger, monumental vessels, further strengthens the impression already gained from the quality of the painted decoration that we are dealing with everyday, household pottery given as simple offerings to the god.[7] We need not give serious consideration, then, to suggestions which claim,

[6] Other excavated Geometric sanctuaries in Greece have also produced large numbers of drinking vessels:

Thebes, Ismenion: A. Keramopoulos, Δελτ. 3, 1917, pp. 66-79.

Kea, Ayia Irini: J. L. Caskey, *Hesperia* 33, 1964, pp. 332-333.

Perachora, Sanctuary of Hera Akraia: H. Payne, *Perachora* I, Oxford, 1940, pp. 53-67.

Tegea, under the temple of Athena Alea: C. Dugas, *B.C.H.* 45, 1921, pp. 404-414.

Sparta, Sanctuary of Artemis Orthia: *J.H.S.*, Suppl. V, *The Sanctuary of Artemis Orthia at Sparta*, 1929, ed. R. M. Dawkins, pp. 54-69.

Sparta, Amyklaion: E. Buschor and W. von Massow, *Ath. Mitt.* 52, 1927, pp. 14-15, 46-53.

Ithaka, Aitos: Sylvia Benton, *B.S.A.* 48, 1953, pp. 260-337.

Chios, Emporio: John Boardman, *B.S.A.*, Suppl. VI, *Excavations in Chios, 1952-5, Greek Emporio*, 1967, pp. 102-147.

[7] There are only a few exceptions: **252** and **270**, from name workshops; also, the oversized vessels: **192-194** (Protogeometric kraters), **199** (one-handled cup), **238** and **239** (skyphoi), **250** (Geometric krater), **251** (oinochoe).

for example, that the offerings were specifically intended to catch the rain water of Zeus,[8] or that because of the high number of drinking vessels there was some sort of drinking ritual involved.[9]

The presence of a quantity of later material in the votive dump suggests that some kind of worship also took place on the top of Hymettos in Late Roman times. The material is mainly lamps, which is not surprising, since they were quite inexpensive and common in all homes.[10] At cave sanctuary sites of this period, such as those at Vari and on Mount Parnes near Phyle, lamps were found in great abundance.[11] No doubt they were used to light the chambers during worship ceremonies, as well as serving as offerings. But on the summit of Mount Hymettos, where there was no question of lighting needs, the lamps must simply represent cheap offerings of the people.

The lamps provide no clues concerning the nature of the worship which took place and very little information about the worshippers themselves. They were apparently pagans since, except for one lamp (**342**), no Christian artifacts were found.[12] Most of the lamps show signs of burning around the nozzle, but this probably means only that they were used at home before being dedicated on the mountain top. Any further comment on the Late Roman activity must await a proper consideration of the nature of the Geometric and Archaic sanctuary.

[8] See W. Wrede, *Attika*, Athens, 1934, p. 12.

[9] Read the thoughts of T. P. Howe and Eva Brann, *T.A.P.A.* 89, 1958, p. 49, note 24, on the high proportion of cups and skyphoi generally in Geometric deposits. The suggestion that they may have served as food bowls as well as drinking vessels is probably correct, considering the scarcity of plates in the Geometric period.

[10] On the use of lamps in ancient Greek sanctuaries, cf. Martin Nilsson, *Opuscula Archaeologica* 6, 1950, pp. 96-111.

[11] Vari: C. Weller and others, *A.J.A.* 7, 1903, pp. 263-349; Mount Parnes: K. Rhomaios, Ἐφ. Ἀρχ., 1906, cols. 89-116.

[12] The material from the Late Roman levels in the Cave of Pan near Phyle is similar. A. Skias, Ἀρχ. Ἐφ., 1918, p. 16, argues persuasively against Rhomaios that the cave was a center for pagan, not Christian, worship.

CHAPTER IV

GENERAL CONCLUSIONS

A. The Religious Background

The worship of Zeus on Hymettos was an acknowledgment of one of his basic aspects, that of weather god. In fact, it was weather phenomena, especially those of a more violent nature, such as thunder and lightning, strong winds, and heavy rains, which gave birth to the very concept of the deity. Spectacular storms with loud thunder claps and dazzling lightning flashes led early man to suppose that a supreme, omnipotent being was responsible for such terrifying and awful happenings. Linguists have derived the name Zeus from an old Indo-European root meaning " shine," and A. B. Cook has constructed an extensive thesis on the origin of Zeus as a god of the bright sky based on this etymology.[1] Martin Nilsson has countered this hypothesis, distrusting the etymology and arguing that man's everyday environment, the bright, blue sky and shining sun, was simply not enough to spawn the belief in a supreme power.[2] Cook cites numerous references in which Zeus is associated with the sun and bright sky, but they are mostly from Classical and later sources. Our chief early source, Homer, on the other hand, frequently casts Zeus in his earlier, basic role of weather god.[3]

This aspect of Zeus was especially important to farmers. Since Zeus was believed to control the fructifying rain needed by their crops, farmers naturally considered him an important agricultural fertility deity. It is uncertain, however, whether or not this connection predated the end of the Bronze Age. Zeus is mentioned in some of the Mycenaean Greek texts, but his nature is obscure. Mother goddesses functioned as fertility deities of vegetation in the Bronze Age, and they often consorted with a male partner, the " boy god ". But again it is unclear whether or not he in turn became the agricultural fertility god Zeus.[4]

After the collapse of Mycenaean civilization and the infusion of new Indo-European elements into the culture, Greek religion evolved and emerged in a more recognizable form. We now clearly see Zeus acknowledged as the supreme god who

[1] *Zeus* I, chapter 1, *passim*.

[2] *Archiv für Religionswissenschaft* 25, 1938, pp. 156-171; *Geschichte der griechischen Religion,* 3rd ed., Munich, 1967, pp. 389-391.

[3] Several of the more common epithets of Zeus found in Homer reflect the deity's role: Lightning-slinger, Thunderer, Cloudgatherer. Precipitation is often called the water of Zeus: e. g. *Iliad* V, 91; XI, 493; XII, 286.

[4] For the opposing view, see E. O. James, *Prehistoric Religion*, London, 1957, pp. 195-201.

ruled from the mountain heights and controlled the weather. It was to him that farmers paid homage. Hesiod provides us with the earliest literary evidence of Zeus' importance for agriculture when he exhorts farmers to pray to Zeus Chthonios and Demeter before beginning the season's first plowing (*Erga*, 465-467). It is interesting that Zeus Chthonios is associated with agriculture here. He is recognized as a god of the soil rather than of the underworld,[5] and his connection with Demeter, guardian of seeds and cultivation, comes naturally.

Important evidence of Zeus' role in agriculture is also obtained from sources of the 5th century B.C., although such information must reflect earlier beliefs. Several Athenian religious festivals paid honor to an agricultural Zeus in the 5th century. They very likely originated much earlier, and their continuation into later times was probably due more to the inherent conservatism of the agricultural population than to any special religious fervor for Zeus. The two most important celebrations, the Diasia festival of Zeus Meilichios and the Dipoleia of Zeus Polieus, both contained an agricultural Zeus as the central figure.[6] But by the latter part of the 5th century these festivals were so diminished in stature that we are forced to conclude that Zeus now played a much reduced role in the rural life of Attica. This may be attributed to three major factors: the growth of Demeter as an important fertility goddess,[7] the rise of local agricultural heroes,[8] and, as Athens became a large city, the evolution of Zeus into an urban deity.

It must be emphasized, however, that Zeus did not surrender his control of the weather. Several authorities testify to this fact, and although somewhat late, they must reflect popular belief which survived from earlier times. Plutarch names Zeus Ombrios as an important agricultural deity (*Moralia* II, 158 E). Marcus Aurelius quotes an Athenian prayer in which Zeus is called upon to rain for the sake of the plowings and fields (*Meditations* V, 7). Finally, Alkiphron describes offerings made to Zeus Hyetios during a period of drought in Attica (*Epistles* II, 33). Thus, despite

[5] At a later date, but in the same capacity, Zeus Chthonios and Ge Chthonie received sacrifices on Mykonos for the success of the crops: *S.I.G.*[3], 1024. For further discussion of the agricultural traits of Zeus Chthonios see A. Fairbanks, *A.J.P.* 21, 1900, pp. 244-249.

[6] L. Deubner, *Attische Feste*, Berlin, 1932, pp. 155-174; T. P. Howe, *A.J.A.* 59, 1955, pp. 296-299.

[7] Demeter was the deity who always watched over the seed as it germinated and grew, and she had festivals all year long: cf. L. Deubner, *op. cit.* (note 6 above), pp. 40-92; M. Nilsson, *Greek Popular Religion*, pp. 24-27. She also seems to have taken over Athena's old agricultural duties. Traces of Athena's role as an agricultural goddess can be seen in the *bouzygion*, the annual sacred plowing under the Acropolis: cf. Jane Harrison and M. deG. Verrall, *Mythology and Monuments of Ancient Athens*, London, 1890, pp. 166-168; R. Schlaifer, *Harv. St. Class. Phil.* 54, 1943, pp. 53-59. See also L. Deubner, *op. cit.* (note 6, above), p. 17, for Athena in the Procharisteria.

[8] For a study of one such hero, see M. Jameson, *T.A.P.A.* 82, 1951, pp. 49-61.

the fact that Demeter came to be regarded as the chief guardian of the crops and soil, Zeus was always looked to for rain which was so necessary for growth.[9]

In a mountainous country such as Greece the tops of mountains were naturally associated with the deity who controlled weather phenomena, since mountain peaks were often shrouded in clouds. The highest peak of a region was often considered sacred to Zeus, and it conveyed weather signs to the surrounding inhabitants.[10]

Not all peak sanctuaries of Zeus were concerned with weather. In the most thorough study on the subject A. B. Cook has collected the evidence for various peaks which were commemorated as the birthplace, marriage-place, death-place, or simply the throne of Zeus.[11] Furthermore, Zeus was commonly worshipped on mountain tops as Hypsistos, Hypatos, or with similar titles by virtue of his status as supreme god among the Olympians. Also, Zeus was quite often given the name of the mountain on which he was worshipped. In most of these cases the god no doubt possessed a dual nature, serving one worshipper as the weather god, another as Supreme Zeus. Only a very few peak sanctuaries in Greece were devoted specifically to Zeus the rain god. Before they are discussed, four others must be briefly considered for which evidence exists or has been interpreted as suggesting that Zeus was worshipped mainly as a rain god at their altars (see Pl. 1).

Oros ("The Mountain"), Aigina. Atop this peak (+ 531 m.), the island's highest mountain, was a sanctuary of Zeus Panhellenios. Isokrates (IX, 14-15) and Pausanias (II, 29, 8) tell the story of Aiakos, mythical king of Aigina, who once offered sacrifices to Zeus on this mountain when all of Greece was suffering from a lack of rain. Afterwards a sanctuary of Zeus Panhellenios was established in gratitude for his ending the drought. Excavations have disclosed the remains of the sanctuary, including a complex part way up the northern slope identified as a hostel and at the very summit a built platform with the altar of Zeus.[12] The religious nature of this sanctuary was undoubtedly broader in scope than that indicated by the probably aetiological Aiakos myth. The monumental architecture establishment and the

---

[9] The same may be said for the Romans and Jupiter, their rain god, and early Christians who believed that God caused and averted rain. For later rain deities, see E. S. McCartney, *C.W.* 18, 1924-1925, pp. 154-157, 163-166; E. Semple, *The Geography of the Mediterranean Region and its Relation to Ancient History,* London, 1932, pp. 505-538.

[10] Hymettos was not the only mountain on which weather signs were identified. Theophrastos notes others in his essay, *de Signis Tempestatum*: clouds on Mount Parnes signaled rain (3, 43); the same held for Oros on Aigina (1, 24) and Mount Athos (2, 34). It was a sign of fair weather if mountain tops in general were free of clouds (3, 51).

[11] *Zeus* I, pp. 124-163; *Zeus* II, Appendix, B, pp. 868-987.

[12] A full report of the Oros excavation never appeared; cf. the brief accounts by A. Furtwängler, *Aegina, Das Heiligtum der Aphaia* I, pp. 473-474; G. Welter, *Arch. Anz.* 33, 1938, cols. 8-16. None of the pottery found at the altar was published, but it was said to range from Geometric through Late Roman times.

epithet of the deity would seem to signify some more important cult center than was necessary for the rain god. But in view of the fact that Oros was regarded as a weather barometer, at least the local population must have been accustomed to using the sanctuary for rain requests.[13]

Sta Marmara, Megara. On a spur of Mount Geraneia a short distance west of the town of Megara was a sanctuary of Zeus Aphesios. Pausanias (I, 44, 9) states that this sanctuary was likewise established after Aiakos had offered sacrifices for rain and that it honored Zeus as the releaser of rain. Lewis Farnell accepted this explanation of the title,[14] but Preller and Robert reject it as aetiological and suggest instead that it means " Escort " or " Patron of the Journey ".[15] A. B. Cook interprets Aphesios to mean " He Who Lets Fly ", connecting it with the hurling of thunderbolts by Zeus.[16] Finally, the *Etymologicum Magnum* (*s. v.* Ἀφέσιος Ζεύς) explains the title as " Savior ". Excavations at the site (+ 503 m.) uncovered the foundations of a temple, an altar, and a complex of other buildings.[17] The remains have been variously interpreted,[18] but to whichever opinion we may choose to give preference, it is evident that this sanctuary functioned as something definitely more than a shrine of the rain god. In all probability the statement of Pausanias is aetiological as Preller and Robert believed.[19]

Mount Lykaion. On this Arkadian mountain was located what was probably the most famous peak sanctuary of Zeus in ancient Greece, that of Zeus Lykaios. Pausanias (VIII, 38, 4) relates that one of the functions of the priest of Zeus Lykaios was to pray to the god for rain whenever the land of Arkadia was suffering from drought. The worship of Zeus Lykaios involved much more, however, and the rain ceremony was performed only when the need arose.[20] The Greek archaeologist Kourouniotis excavated the altar (+ 1400 m.) and discovered that it was simply

[13] In more recent times also the islanders were in the habit of predicting rain from the gathering of clouds on Oros. Furthermore, a ceremony involving an ikon in the monastery of the Panagia on the north side of the mountain was believed to bring rain: cf. J. P. Harland, *Prehistoric Aigina*, Paris, 1925, p. 84, and *Studies in Honor of Ullman*, St. Louis, 1960, pp. 17-18.

[14] *The Cults of the Greek States* I, Oxford, 1896, p. 51.

[15] *Griechische Mythologie*, Berlin, 1894, p. 118, note 3.

[16] *Zeus* II, pp. 179-180.

[17] D. Philios, Ἐφ. Ἀρχ., 1890, cols. 21-56.

[18] Philos believed that the large structure near the temple was a priest's quarters. H. Lolling, Ἐφ. Ἀρχ., 1887, cols. 213-216, was of the opinion that the structure was a private dwelling to which a sanctuary was later attached. A. B. Cook, *Zeus* II, Appendix, B, pp. 895-897, thought that some of the rooms were for incubation and some connected with a chthonic cult.

[19] It is doubtful that Pausanias even visited the sanctuary. He states that it is located on the very top of the mountain, though in fact it is situated on a level area well below the top. The view from the sanctuary overlooks a fertile agricultural district west of Megara and most of the Saronic Gulf. Of the remains themselves little is to be seen today.

[20] All the evidence is collected in Cook, *Zeus* I, pp. 63-99.

a mound of ash, pottery, and animal bones on a flat, circular platform hewn from the rock. This immense mound formed the apex of the main peak.[21] The finds were disappointingly meager, dating mainly from the 5th and 4th centuries B.C.

It is interesting to note the similarities between the sanctuary of Zeus Lykaios and that of Zeus Panhellenios on Aigina. Both consisted of a lower precinct and an altar on a flat platform at the summit.[22] Along with the altar of Zeus on Hymettos they fit well into Cook's first stage of mountain-top worship to Zeus, the dedication of a simple altar with neither temple nor statue of the god.[23] The altars on Hymettos and Oros show that this stage was prevalent at least from the Protogeometric to the Archaic period, while the altar of Zeus Lykaios is a notably later example.[24]

Mount Pelion. We are informed by a fragment of Dikaiarchos that Zeus Aktaios had a sanctuary on Pelion.[25] No mention is made of a rain ceremony, but one has been inferred from a curious ritual which took place there. On a very hot summer's day a procession of men clad in sheepskins would ascend to the sanctuary of Zeus and make offerings. This ceremony has been interpreted in two different ways: the men were trying to assimilate themselves to Zeus the ram god, or they were imitating the fleecy clouds of Zeus in order to induce rainfall.[26] In fact, these are only educated guesses about an ancient religious custom whose real meaning we may never know. A partial excavation at the sanctuary (+ 1635 m.) turned up little useful evidence.[27]

Of the four sanctuaries considered, those on Oros and Mount Lykaion definitely received offerings for rain, while those on Mount Pelion and Sta Marmara possibly did. Some fifty or more other mountain-top sanctuaries of Zeus in Greece are mentioned in ancient literature, but at how many of these Zeus was worshipped as a rain god is impossible to determine. It is doubtful that excavations would be of much help in identifying many sanctuaries of the rain god, since in most cases, as we have seen with the sanctuary on Mount Hymettos, the ritual was fairly simple and

[21] Ἐφ. Ἀρχ., 1904, cols. 153-214, especially cols. 163-164.

[22] In contrast to Lykaion, however, G. Welter, *Aigina*, Berlin, 1938, p. 91, believed that a marble altar stood on top of Oros. Pieces of coarse-grained white marble, apparently not native to the mountain, are strewn about the top. They may be remains of an altar.

[23] *Zeus* I, pp. 117-123. The second stage was the introduction of an image of the deity to the top of the mountain, and the third the housing of the image in a temple.

[24] G. Mylonas, in *Classical Studies in Honor of William A. Oldfather*, Urbana, Ill., 1943, pp. 122-133, argues unconvincingly that the cult originated on Mount Lykaion in Mycenaean times. The earliest object found at the site was a single bronze figurine of the 7th century B.C.

[25] For this reference, see Cook, *Zeus* II, Appendix, B, p. 869, note 2.

[26] Cf. Cook, *Zeus* I, pp. 420-421; *Zeus* III, pp. 31-32.

[27] The excavation was carried out by Arvanitopoullos whose report appeared in Πρακτικά, 1911, pp. 305-312. But Cook quotes a letter (*Zeus* III, p. 1161, Addendum to vol. II, p. 896, note 2) by a traveler who visited the site and described much of the report as pure fabrication.

the offerings unrevealing. Votive pottery is rarely distinctive as to a particular trait of a deity, and inscribed dedications are customarily all too brief, giving the name of the god and dedicant but little else. If a large number of peak sanctuaries of Zeus were excavated and published, perhaps some feature common to them all could be construed as befitting Zeus the rain god,[28] but until we possess such a volume of data, our only recourse is to conjecture. Even so, we would probably not be far wrong in maintaining that a great many of Zeus' peak altars served the local population for rain offerings. Although rain came fairly regularly, it could not be counted on to come at the right time and in sufficient amounts each year to insure a good harvest. Thus, worship of Zeus the rain god must have taken place on certain peaks in every neighborhood.[29]

Two titles by which Zeus was sometimes identified, Ombrios (Showery) and Hyetios (Rainy) leave no doubt that this was how he was worshipped in specific instances. The two titles were synonymous,[30] and there was no preference in the use of one over the other. They occur frequently enough to demonstrate the widespread attention given to this aspect of Zeus in Greece, although it is somewhat surprising to learn how seldom they are connected with Zeus on mountain tops.[31] Aside from Hymettos, the only other mountain in Greece known to have a sanctuary of Zeus Ombrios was nearby Parnes.[32] No mountain-top sanctuaries of Zeus Hyetios are known in Greece, and only one peak outside Greece was associated with him, Mount Tmolos near Sardis.[33]

The evidence indicates instead that Zeus the rain god could be worshipped anywhere, not just on mountain tops. The ancient city of Elis is reported to have had a sanctuary of Zeus Ombrios, but no mention is made of it being on a mountain.[34] Pausanias tells us that there were altars of Zeus Hyetios at Argos (II, 19, 8) and in the grove of Trophonios at Lebadeia (IX, 39, 4). Zeus Hyetios is further attested

[28] In the precinct on Mount Lykaion, for example, was found a group of figurines of Zeus hurling a thunderbolt. These quite appropriately serve as offerings to Zeus as a god of weather or rain.

[29] Cf. M. Nilsson, *Greek Popular Religion*, pp. 5-8.

[30] They were considered so in later times and must have been in earlier periods as well. Nonnos, *Dionysiaca* XIII, 522-544, equates Zeus Hyetios with Zeus Brombios, surely a scribal error for Ombrios. Plutarch names Zeus Ombrios as one of the chief agricultural deities (*Moralia* II, 158 E), whereas Themistios accords Zeus Hyetios the same function (*Orations* XXX, 349a), Hesychios equates Ὕης (*s.v.*) with Zeus Ombrios, although the Suda (*s.v.*) and Photios (*s.v.*), quoting Kleidemos, explain it as an epithet of Dionysos.

[31] All of the evidence for Zeus Ombrios and Zeus Hyetios is collected in Cook, *Zeus* III, pp. 525-570. Although he ranges too far afield, Cook's long discussion on Zeus and rain, *Zeus* III, pp. 284-881, is the most thorough study on the subject.

[32] This sanctuary is discussed more fully in Appendix B.

[33] I. Lydus, *de Mensibus* IV, 48, written *ca.* A.D. 530.

[34] Scholium to Lykophron, *Alexandria*, 160.

in inscriptions on Kos and Rhodes, but again there is no evidence for an association with mountain tops.[35] For Zeus Ombrios the epigraphical evidence consists of two small, fragmentary altars in the Athenian Agora,[36] and a private dedication at Corinth.[37]

The placement of a sanctuary of Zeus the rain god within a city or in cultivable fields is easy to understand. It would be located near the crops, and the god's attention could easily be drawn to those areas which needed rain the most. Small shrines of Zeus Ombrios and Zeus Hyetios may have been quite common about the Greek countryside, in contrast to their apparent absence from mountain tops.

On mountains Zeus probably served multiple functions. It was thus deemed inappropriate and unnecessary to favor one aspect of Zeus over another by giving him a specific title. The most appropriate solution was to name Zeus after the particular mountain on which he was worshipped. In this way he could be honored equally well as the rain god and Supreme Zeus. We should not, therefore, really expect to find sanctuaries of Zeus Ombrios and Zeus Hyetios located on mountains. Our evidence agrees well with this conclusion, with the notable exception of the sanctuaries of Zeus Ombrios on Hymettos and Parnes. Their location may have been prompted by the fact that these mountains were regarded as weather indicators. Other peaks displayed similar weather signs, but in all of Greece only the signs on Hymettos and Parnes were considered significant enough to merit acknowledgment with sanctuaries of Zeus the rain god. Other factors, such as chronological considerations, may have played some part in the distribution and location of sanctuaries of Zeus Ombrios and Zeus Hyetios, but the evidence is insufficient to test these possibilities.

A discussion of the worship for rain in ancient Greece should also touch upon the subject of rain magic. First of all, a distinction must be made between rain magic and worship for rain. The latter, as it took place on Mount Hymettos, involved simply the offering of gifts and sacrifices to the rain god in hopes of inducing rain. The former was centered around some ritual which it was believed would magically produce rain. Rain magic was practiced, for example, on Mount

[35] An altar of Zeus Hyetios on Kos: W. Patton and E. Hicks, *The Inscriptions of Cos*, Oxford, 1891, pp. 269-270, no. 382, lines 28-29, of the 3rd century B.C.; a sanctuary on Rhodes: A. Maiuri, *Annuario* VIII-IX, 1925-1926, p. 321, no. 4 from the Roman Imperial period.

[36] Originally published as fragments of three separate altars by A. E. Raubitschek, *Hesperia* 12, 1943, pp. 72-73, nos. 19-21. Two of the pieces were later found to join: *Hesperia* 37, 1968, p. 291, no. 32. The altar fragments were all found in disturbed contexts, but in antiquity they must have been located in or near the Agora. They date to *ca.* A.D. 100.

[37] B. D. Meritt, *Corinth*, VIII, i, *Greek Inscriptions, 1896-1927*, Cambridge, Mass., 1931, p. 72, no. 102 (= *I.G.* IV, 1598). This Late Roman monument is a circular drum of white marble which originally bore a Latin inscription. For its later use as a dedication to Zeus Ombrios, R. L. Scranton, *Corinth*, I, iii, *Monuments in the Lower Agora and North of the Archaic Temple*, Princeton, 1951, p. 146, believes that the cuttings on top indicate that it carried a large bronze statue with left foot advanced. It must have stood near where the drum was found, southwest of the Propylaia.

Lykaion where, according to Pausanias (VIII, 38, 4), the priest of Zeus used an oak branch to stir up the dust which then fell back to earth as rain. Many other magical ceremonies were believed to cause rain, and the practice of rain magic appears to have been common in ancient Greece.[38]

This conclusion was countered long ago by C. H. Morgan, who rightly attacked the tendency prevalent at the time of seeing a more widespread use of rain magic than was justified by the evidence.[39] Morgan's conclusion, that rain magic was not common in the best periods of Greek culture, suffers, however, from his failure to make the distinction between rain magic and worship for rain, and his neglect of the abundant evidence for simple acts of rain magic. When considering only the literary evidence it is rather meager. But Gruppe's collection of the evidence for magic rites, fetishes, and symbols connected with rain is impressive and shows that rain magic was more common than Morgan thought. Rain was not a constant preoccupation with the ancient Greeks, but let there be just a brief period of insufficient rainfall and a great many people would resort to superstitious and magical means of causing rain. There may even have been rain-magic practices at small sanctuaries such as that on Hymettos, but the archaeological evidence would not show this.

We cannot conclude this discussion without briefly considering worship for rain in the Mycenaean era and the group of Mycenaean potsherds found in the Hymettos excavation. In the preceding chapter these sherds were dissociated from the sanctuary because of the small quantity involved. A further consideration leading us to doubt any connection between the Mycenaean material and the sanctuary is the fact that there are no known peak sanctuaries of the Mycenaean period in Greece.[40] In sharp contrast to Crete, whose mountain peaks yield abundant evidence of the vital role they played in Minoan religion,[41] the mountains of mainland Greece have

[38] See the thorough discussion by Otto Gruppe, *Griechische Mythologie und Religionsgeschichte* II, Munich, 1906, pp. 818-834.

[39] *T.A.P.A.* 32, 1901, pp. 83-109. A good later example of the tendency which Morgan warned against was occasioned by the publication of a Geometric fragment from Kynosarges by Droop, *B.S.A.* 12, 1905-1906, p. 82, fig. 2b. The fragment has a scene done by a painter of the Rattle Group (Coldstream, *G.G.P.*, pp. 71-72), which Jane Harrison, *Themis*, Cambridge, 1912, pp. 76-79, interpreted as a rain-making ritual. J. M. Cook, *B.C.H.* 70, 1946, pp. 97-101, proved that the scene depicts a graveside ritual and has nothing to do with rain making. Coldstream, *op. cit.*, lists other examples; the latest published example of the scene: S. McNally, *A.J.A.* 73, 1969, pp. 459-464.

[40] For a survey of Mycenaean sanctuaries, see R. Hägg, *Opuscula Atheniensia* 8, 1968, pp. 39-59.

[41] The evidence for Minoan peak sites is presented by Paul Faure, *B.C.H.* 91, 1967, pp. 115-133; 93, 1969, pp. 174-194, and 96, 1972, pp. 390-402. The nature of peak worship in Minoan Crete is disputed: see the lively debate between B. C. Dietrich, *Historia* 18, 1969, pp. 257-275; 20, 1971, pp. 513-523, and B. Rutkowski, *Historia* 20, 1971, pp. 1-19. For Zeus on Cretan peaks, see Cook, *Zeus* II, Appendix, B, pp. 925-948; also P. Faure, *B.C.H.* 91, 1967, pp. 129-132. R. F. Willetts, *Cretan Cults and Festivals*, London, 1962, pp. 231-251, collects all the evidence for the

produced hardly any Bronze Age material. With the exceptions of Hymettos, Oros, and Ayios Elias at Mycenae, there are almost no Mycenaean remains of any sort known to me on Greek peaks.[42] Yet even more dramatic *argumenta e silentio* have in the past been shown to be merely the result of inadequate exploration, so we must avoid a categorical statement on the matter. There may have existed Mycenaean mountain-top sanctuaries, and the Mycenaean sherds from Hymettos may in fact have had some religious significance. But in view of the strength of the negative evidence and the vast differences separating Mycenaean from later Greek religion, we are safer in assuming no religious activity on the top of Mount Hymettos in the Bronze Age.[43]

B. HISTORICAL CONSIDERATIONS

As has been shown, the sanctuary of Zeus on Hymettos functioned during the Protogeometric, Geometric, Archaic, and Late Roman periods. None of the pottery of these periods may be dismissed as unexplained or accidental, because the quantity from each is too great. Instead, a hypothesis must be developed which satisfactorily explains why Zeus was worshipped on Hymettos during these particular periods and not in others. The explanation favored here is that activity at that sanctuary was a reflection of the agricultural history of Attica. Rain was of paramount importance at times when the Attic citizenry was dependent for its food on the soil of Attica itself. In other periods, when most of the food was imported, the main concern was with keeping the trade routes open for the cargo ships. When the former situation prevailed, a mountain-top sanctuary of Zeus should receive large numbers of offerings

worship of Zeus in Crete. There is no clear indication tht he was ever worshipped specifically as a rain god anywhere on the island.

[42] In addition to the top, the slopes of Hymettos have also yielded some Mycenaean pottery apparently from settlements. The evidence is mainly in the sherd collection of the British School of Archaeology in Athens, and consists of L.H. IIIA–B sherd material from sites just west and south of Kaisariani monastery: cf. *J.H.S.* 87, 1967, p. 183. On Oros there was a curious Late Helladic settlement around the summit: cf. G. Welter, *Arch. Anz.* 33, 1938, col. 14. At Mycenae Wace excavated a small fort on the summit of Mount Ayios Elias: *B.S.A.* 25, 1921-1923, pp. 429-434. Recently, members of the Argolid Exploration Project found L.H. IIIA–B pottery on the peak of Profitis Elias near Kranidi. The material, consisting mainly of kylix and deep-bowl fragments, was found strewn about the small summit. Medieval pottery and a dry rubble enceinte were also noted. Perhaps this high hill was the acropolis of Homeric Mases just to the west on the bay of Koilada. For the opportunity to examine this material I am grateful to M. H. Jameson and J. A. Dengate. Furthermore, it must be noted that Mycenaean peak sanctuaries are often inferred, but from evidence of dubious value. Representations on Mycenaean seals of a deity standing on a mound or stepped platform are invariably interpreted as scenes of mountain-top worship. And in a recent study Chrysoula Kardara has ingeniously argued that the Mycenaeans built sanctuaries with free-standing columns on mountain tops in order to attract the lightning god: ’Αρχ. ’Εφ., 1966, pp. 149-200, especially pp. 176-181. Again, her arguments are based on seal representations. But where is the physical evidence for all this? There is none.

[43] This still leaves the Mycenaean material unexplained, and I admit to having no plausible solution.

for rain, while in the latter it would tend to lie neglected. To test the validity of this hypothesis the provisioning of Attica, and especially Athens, with food must be discussed. It will essentially be a question of the grain supply, since grain was the basic component of the diet.

There is no good reason not to believe that within two generations of the collapse of Mycenaean civilization settled conditions prevailed once again throughout Greece. The advanced stages of the Protogeometric pottery style are enough to indicate this. That the cultivation of grain crops formed the economic basis of this stability seems also quite certain. Grazing stock was important as a source of wool and milk, but arable agriculture was far more important, because it provided the bulk of the food supply of grain. This was probably just as true for the Bronze Age as for the Iron Age,[44] although good evidence does not really begin to appear before the 9th century B.C.

The evidence we do have comes mainly from graves in the Athenian Agora and Kerameikos which contain clay models of granaries. The most impressive in the series, a unique chest with five model granaries on its lid, was found in an Agora grave dating from the final years of the Early Geometric period, ca. 850 B.C.[45] This and most of the other graves containing granaries were rich in other finds, and some contained objects from foreign lands as well. It was not trade or foreign contacts that was responsible for the wealth exhibited by these graves, however. Instead, the model granaries are a good indication that much of the wealth came from the land in the form of grain.

The Agora burial with the unique chest is that of a woman who obviously belonged to the landed aristocracy. The aristocratic class must certainly have been determined by birth at this time, but it is interesting to consider the possibility that

[44] T. P. Howe, *T.A.P.A.* 89, 1958, pp. 46-55, has gathered the evidence which suggests that grain was only a supplement to the Mycenaean diet. In part, her arguments are based on negative evidence which could yet be altered by future discoveries. The absence of bake ovens and granaries at Mycenaean sites is striking, but their discovery perhaps awaits the excavation of more Mycenaean towns like Lefkandi in Euboia where a number of grain-storage bins were found in the L.H. IIIC levels: cf. M. R. Popham and L. H. Sackett, *Excavations at Lefkandi, Euboea: 1964-66*, London, 1968, p. 12, fig. 14 and p. 15, fig. 21. The absence of ovens might also be explained by postulating that the Mycenaeans cultivated barley much more than wheat. This has been argued convincingly for Messenia and is probably true for the rest of Bronze Age Greece as well: see *The Minnesota Messenia Expedition,* edd. Wm. McDonald and G. Rapp, Jr., Minneapolis, 1972, chapter 11, by H. von Wersch. Barley does not make good bread, but is used for porridge and mash, which do not require ovens. The suggestion that the Mycenaeans may have imported grain is rightly denied by G. Mylonas, *Mycenae and the Mycenaean Age*, Princeton, 1966, pp. 210-211. Some My-cenaean agricultural tools have been found in Greece: plowshares, cf. H. W. Catling, *Cypriote Bronzework in the Mycenaean World,* Oxford, 1964, p. 81; tanged sickles, cf. Catling, *op. cit.,* p. 84, note 7.

[45] See E. L. Smithson, *Hesperia* 37, 1968, pp. 77-116, and especially p. 92, note 41 for other model granaries in Attic Geometric graves. Regarding these objects I agree fully with Smithson that they are models of granaries.

our deceased lady was also ranked in some fashion according to the extent and production of her family's land holdings. It has even been suggested that the five model granaries on the chest are a symbol of the landed class to which the lady belonged, the *pentakosiomedimnoi*.[46] The existence of social classes defined solely by land holdings is anachronistic for the period of the Agora burial, but it is possible that within the aristocracy social classes based on landed wealth were already forming.

Whatever importance model granaries from Attic Geometric graves may have regarding early landed classes, they are also invaluable in revealing to us the agricultural orientation of Attica in the Iron Age. The models must be copies of actual large granaries which were situated about the countryside for the storage of grain.[47] Already by the Early Geometric period, to conclude from the Agora models, grain crops were being profitably cultivated in Attica. This success stemmed from a long period of development and recovery following the collapse of Mycenaean civilization. The Protogeometric period ushered in this era of recovery, and by the end of that period a large majority of the Attic population was seriously engaged in arable agriculture.

If the above is a valid statement, the presence of Late Protogeometric pottery at the sanctuary of Zeus may be explained. This was a time long before the importation of grain, when the population relied solely on cultivable land in Attica for its food supply. Under these circumstances it would be natural to see the people taking some measures in their religious practices which reflected a concern with rain. We know very little about the religious customs of the Protogeometric period,[48] but there can be no other reason, I believe, for the commencement of offerings on Hymettos towards the end of that period than such a connection with aration agriculture. Offerings were made to the rain god Zeus for the sake of the crops.

During the two centuries of the Geometric period which followed, agriculture flourished in Attica, as did worship at the Hymettos sanctuary. Notable omissions appear to occur in the Early and Middle Geometric periods, but large numbers of offerings were made during the latter part of the Middle and the entire Late Geometric periods, reflecting the large-scale cultivation of the land.[49]

[46] Smithson, *op. cit.* (note 45, above), pp. 96-97. Alternatively, the model granaries represent a part of the food supply required by the deceased on the journey to the underworld: cf. H. A. Thompson and R. E. Wycherley, *The Athenian Agora,* XIV, *The Agora of Athens*, Princeton, 1972, p. 13.

[47] The nearest physical remains to such hypothetical structures that I know of are the so-called theta structures at Lefkandi: rf. M. R. Popham and L. H. Sackett, *op. cit.* (note 44, above), pp. 30-31. The function of these structures, which preserve only foundations, is problematical. They could have had to do with olive or grape pressing, or they could be the foundations of granaries.

[48] Aside from the information obtained from graves regarding funerary customs, we can point to only one certain Protogeometric sanctuary in Attica, a sacrificial pyre containing over 200 pots, located in the area of the Academy of Plato: Ph. Stavropoullos, Πρακτικά, 1958, pp. 8-9.

[49] A possible prolonged drought in the later 8th century B.C. may have been partly responsible

The crop did not come easily. The land was subjected to extensive cultivation in order to provide adequately for the needs of Athens and other growing communities.[50] Attic soil is not very suitable for grain crops, and without such modern aids as hybrid grains and chemical fertilizers, the only way to increase grain production was to increase the acreage under cultivation. By Late Geometric times much of the available land was planted with crops.[51] And without the convenience of modern irrigation methods, the farmers of these early periods were constantly anxious for regular and adequate rainfall. Perhaps the populace would not starve to death if the rainfall was deficient for a short time, but everyone wanted to try to prevent any crop failure due to a lack of rain. Thus, people went regularly with offerings to the sanctuary of Zeus on Hymettos.

We must now consider a different view on the subject of early agriculture which, if correct, would invalidate any attempt to associate with it activity at the Hymettos sanctuary. T. P. Howe has argued that agriculture did not really have its beginnings in Greece until *ca.* 700 B.C., when Hesiod first began writing.[52] Before this, the food supply is seen as having come from grazing flocks much as in Mycenaean times. Gradually the pasturage is supposed to have become inadequate, necessitating a change in food habits. Such a work as Hesiod's *Erga*, Howe believes, would not have been written except at a time when crops were first beginning to be widely cultivated. Not only does the archaeological evidence run counter to Howe's arguments, but Hesiod's poem may be given a different interpretation which admits it to a place in a long-established agricultural community.

Above all must be emphasized a fact which is quite often forgotten about Hesiod's work: its scope. He was writing for his fellow countrymen of rural Boiotia, not for Greeks everywhere. Furthermore, he wrote at a time which saw the beginning of large-scale commercial ventures overseas. The *Erga*, if taken with these considerations in mind, is seen not as a handbook for the initial attempts at agriculture, but an admonition to Boiotian farmers to avoid risky commercial ventures and a reassurance that their way of life, inherited from generations of agricultural forefathers, was the best.[53] Hesiod makes not a single mention of stock grazing. He simply compiles all agrarian knowledge known to him. This was not

for the very large amount of Late Geometric and Early Archaic pottery found at the sanctuary. A drought is suggested by the fact that a large number of wells in the Agora were closed at this time: cf. *Agora* VIII, p. 108.

[50] Graves and wells indicate that Athens especially was becoming populous by the Late Geometric period: cf. *Agora* VIII, p. 108; Coldstream, *G.G.P.*, p. 360.

[51] Late Geometric settlement patterns reveal a large rise in the rural population, which suggests extensive cultivation of Attic soil: Coldstream, *G.G.P.*, pp. 360-362.

[52] *T.A.P.A.* 89, 1958, pp. 44-65. Much the same view is held by A. M. Snodgrass, *The Dark Age of Greece*, Edinburgh, 1971, pp. 378-380.

[53] The Boiotians heeded this advice, as the ceramic evidence indicates: cf. Coldstream, *G.G.P.*, pp. 367-368.

only a useful service, but a necessary one, too, since this traditional vocation was being threatened by other economic enterprises.[54]

While the Boiotians clung to their agricultural way of life, the people of Attica did likewise. Athens was in no hurry to establish overseas colonies, so she must still have been self-sufficient and in no need of food imports or cultivable foreign soil in the 8th and 7th centuries B.C. Contacts, especially with the East, were becoming plentiful, but there is no indication that the basic economic structure at home was in any way altered. Home-grown grain continued to be as crucial as ever. But a terrific strain was exerted on the land in order to maintain self-sufficiency. Clearly time would tell against this situation. Not only would the soil become exhausted and less productive, since the practice of crop rotation was not followed, but more important, the population would outgrow the capability of the land to support it. Imports of foreign grain would then provide the only relief. It is not known for certain when the first shiploads of foreign grain arrived in Attica, but as the circumstances just described must have steadily worsened the agricultural predicament during the course of the 7th century B.C., it is likely that the initial grain imports began at the end of the 7th or beginning of the 6th century.[55]

For the history of the Attic economy at this time we have little direct evidence, but from the agrarian crisis which came to a head in the early 6th century, we may construct a fairly plausible account.[56] The crisis was precipitated largely by the importation of grain. Before imports began, the grain of Attica was in great demand, and many Attic farmers were able to earn a living even on small parcels of land by growing grain for their neighbors in town. But as soon as foreign grain became available, small-time Attic farmers were quickly in trouble, for they could not compete with the more plentiful foreign product and still make ends meet. Their only recourse was to borrow heavily each year from their wealthier neighbors. Many were even forced to put up their own persons as security for loans. Real slavery followed for a number of these farmers, as they were not able to pay back their debts. They greatly resented their unhappy lot and were near to revolt when Solon was chosen to solve the crisis. This he attempted to do by canceling the oppressive debts and reorienting the agricultural basis of Attica from grain crops to the olive and the vine.[57]

[54] A good general analysis of Hesiod's poem is given by T. A. Sinclair, *Hesiod, Works and Days*, London, 1932.

[55] The early Attic colony of Sigeion on the Hellespont founded *ca.* 600 B.C. reflects the growing attention paid by Athenians to overseas grain sources.

[56] This has been attempted by A. French: *Cl. Quart.*, N. S. 6, 1956, pp. 11-25; *Growth of the Athenian Economy*, London, 1964, pp. 10-29. French has been severely criticized for too readily using modern economic theory to explain the developments in Attica in the 7th century B.C. But if French does not always view the situation in its proper perspective, he at least correctly identifies the basic causes of the crisis, in my opinion.

[57] The evidence for dating Solon's archonship to 594/3 B.C. is too well known to need repeating. I remain unconvinced by C. Hignett's attempt, *A History of the Athenian Constitution*, Oxford,

It is uncertain to what extent the planting of olive trees and vines encroached upon the arable land of Attica, but it is not likely that the acreage devoted to cereal crops was seriously curtailed. Vines and olive trees were planted especially on newly claimed land,[58] and olive trees and grains were probably intercultivated much as they are in Greece today. And even after Solon, grain crops continued to be widely cultivated in Attica. But these local grains lost their critical importance as imported grain came to supply the bulk of the food requirements. The Attic crop now formed only a supplement to the people's needs.

These developments in the Attic economy must have had an effect on the people's religious practices. As the importance of Attic grain declined, so preoccupation with the rain god accordingly declined. This is surely reflected in the activity at the sanctuary of Zeus on Mount Hymettos. The large percentage of offerings made in the 7th century should relate to the efforts of farmers to extract enough grain from the soil of Attica to feed the expanding population. The sharp drop in offerings in the 6th century may roughly correspond to the steadily increasing amounts of grain imports and the growing diversification of the local agricultural economy. People were becoming more concerned with the overseas grain sources and trade routes, and they worried less about local rainfall and the Attic harvests. Olive trees and vines are not completely drought resistant, but they could be counted on to produce satisfactory yields under normal Attic weather conditions. Thus the sanctuary of Zeus on Hymettos, which was devoted primarily to the rain god, almost totally ceased to function.

Once foreign grain came to satisfy the dietary requirements of Athens, there was rarely a time when enough food was lacking. The history of the grain supply of Classical and Hellenistic Athens has been the subject of much research and need not be retraced here. But it is worth stressing just how important foreign grain was. For centuries to come following the first food imports, one of the principal considerations guiding much of Athens' foreign policy was the grain supply.[59] Good

---

1952, pp. 316-321, to date Solon's reforms some twenty years after his archonship, even though forceful arguments have recently been put forward for dating both to the 570's: cf. Molly Miller, *Arethusa* 2, 1969, pp. 62-81. For a recent restatement of the case for the earlier date, cf. Malcolm F. McGregor, " Solon's Archonship: The Epigraphic Evidence," in *Polis and Imperium, Studies in Honor of Edward Togo Salmon*, Toronto, 1974, pp. 31-34.

[58] This was first put forward as a suggestion by A. Jardé, *Les céréales dans l'antiquité grecque*, Paris, 1925, pp. 101-105. Since then, studies of aerial photographs have proven this suggestion correct. Especially on Hymettos the slopes were made usable by terracing: cf. John Bradford, *Antiquaries Journal* 36, 1956, pp. 172-180, and *Ancient Landscapes. Studies in Field Archaeology*, London, 1957, pp. 29-34, and pls. 7-8. The slopes of other mountains and hills in Attica were probably heavily terraced for farming as well.

[59] See J. Hasebroek, *Trade and Politics in Ancient Greece*, English translation by L. M. Fraser and D. C. Macgregor, London, 1933. Hasebroek rejects trade as the main factor in the commercial policies of the ancient Greek states, favoring instead the supplying of necessities as the chief consideration. His conclusion is much too extreme, although for Athens the supply of food did

relations were established and maintained with the major grain-producing areas: Pontus, Egypt, Cyrene, and Sicily. We do know of times when natural disasters or political circumstances led to severe grain shortages,[60] but there is no record that in any of these cases the shortage was so prolonged as to force the citizens to turn back to their own land for their basic sustenance. This would have been a measure of extreme desperation, because the population had long since outstripped the capability of the land to feed it adequately. Fortunately such a move never really had to be contemplated, since Athens enjoyed the kindness of a large number of foreign benefactors who readily bestowed gifts of grain on the city in times of shortage.[61]

The situation changed little during the Roman period. Measures taken by the government and generous private donations continued to spare Athens the consequences of a prolonged food shortage.[62] The hoplite general saw to it that the grain supply was adequate, and a special grain treasury existed for the purchase of grain.[63] Beyond this we are poorly informed. We hear nothing of private enterprise in connection with the grain supply, probably because the matter was so critical that the state had assumed full responsibility for obtaining the grain. Two emperors, Hadrian and Constantine, are known to have presented Athens with annual gifts of grain,[64] and others must have done likewise, reasoning that it was far better to undergo the expense of keeping the Eastern provinces well fed than to save the effort but be faced with widespread food riots.

It seems unlikely, then, that Athens ever went hungry for an extended period of time in the Roman era, despite numerous misfortunes which beset the city. There was even a certain degree of prosperity, thanks no doubt to the fact that regular grain shipments were coming in.[65]

occupy a prominent place. Aristotle (*Ath. Pol.* 43, 4) informs us that the first session of each prytany had as one of its main orders of business the question περὶ σίτου, and Demosthenes, especially in the *Orations* XXXII, XXXIV, and XXXV, gives an account of the busy grain-trading activities at Athens. For a thorough study of the grain supply at Athens, see F. Heichelheim in *R.E.*, Suppl. VI, *s.v.* sitos, cols. 819-892; see also M. Rostovtzeff, *The Social and Economic History of the Hellenistic World* I, Oxford, 1941, pp. 74-125.

[60] For food shortages at Athens, see Rostovtzeff, *op. cit.* (note 59, above), III, p. 1329, note 29, and p. 1354, note 41.

[61] The list of Athenian inscriptions conferring honors on foreign benefactors for gifts of grain to the city is long: cf. Heichelheim, *op. cit* (note 59, above), cols. 840-844.

[62] The basic study of the Athenian economy during the Roman period, with frequent reference to the grain supply, is by John Day, *An Economic History of Athens under Roman Domination*, New York, 1942.

[63] On the hoplite general, see D. Geagan, *Hesperia*, Suppl. XII, *The Athenian Constitution after Sulla*, 1967, pp. 18-31. This magistrate also had a connection with the grain supply before the Roman period. For the grain treasury, cf. *ibid.*, p. 22, note 39.

[64] Hadrian's annual dole: Cassius Dio, LXIX, 16, 2. Julian (*Orations* I, 8d) writes that Constantine gave tens of thousands of bushels of wheat annually to Athens.

[65] Archaeology has done much to cast a more favorable light on the economic situation of Roman Athens. For example, the Herulian invasion in A.D. 267 is commonly thought to have

The founding of Constantinople in A.D. 324 did much to alter the economic situation in the East, and much for the worse as far as Athens was concerned. Athens was pre-eminent among cities of the Eastern Empire. Although Peiraieus had been superseded by other Eastern ports, it was still an important commercial center. Also, the university attracted much renown to the city. No other Eastern city could compete with Athens for distinction, and successive emperors made certain that she was well supplied with food. But when Constantine built his Eastern capital on the Bosporos, attention at once shifted away from Athens to the new city. The most immediate effect was seen on Athens' grain supply. Constantinople grew quickly and soon came to require almost all of the grain from Athens' remaining sources.[66] The emperors now holding court in Constantinople were, nevertheless, well disposed to Greece and took special measures for the provisioning of Athens.[67]

Our sources tell us nothing of any serious grain shortages in Athens during the 4th century after Christ or later, but there is one period when a shortage may well have occurred, at the end of the 4th and beginning of the 5th centuries. In A.D. 395 the emperor Theodosius I died and, as he willed it, the empire was officially split between his two sons, Arcadius receiving the eastern half, Honorius the western half. The two brothers soon came under the influence of ambitious ministers at their respective courts and fell to scheming against each other. Also at this time the Visigoth Alaric descended upon Greece from the Balkans, leading his band of Goths on a sweeping campaign which even included sieges of Constantinople and Athens. It seems highly unlikely that Arcadius, fully occupied with these troubles, as well as serious internal disorders at his own court, would have given much thought to the supplying of Greece with grain. Without such attention, Athens received very little foreign grain by her own efforts.[68] This brought about the prospect of a serious food shortage, and the city had no other option but to turn to the soil of Attica for its food.

---

plunged the city into a deep economic depression from which it never really recovered. Evidence from the Athenian Agora, however, shows that the invasion had few detrimental effects on Athenian industry: cf. *Agora* V, p. 3; *Agora* VII, pp. 11, 20-21. Many private individuals appear to have suffered great personal losses due to the invasion (cf. E. Harrison, *The Athenian Agora*, I, *Portrait Sculpture*, Princeton, 1953, pp. 90-92), but economically the city recovered quickly. This it could not have done had food been in short supply for very long.

[66] See Eunapius, *Vit. Soph.*, 462. Constantine began a bread dole at Constantinople for 80,000 recipients, and the number was later increased: cf. A. H. M. Jones, *The Later Roman Empire, A.D. 284-602* III, Oxford, 1964, p. 215, note 20 for the sources. Further on the grain supply of Constantinople, cf. J. L. Teall, *Dumbarton Oaks Papers* XIII, 1959, pp. 89-139, especially pp. 91-96. Teall estimates (pp. 134-135) that the population of Constantinople was in the neighborhood of 500,000 by A.D. 400.

[67] Constantine's large dole of grain to Athens has already been mentioned (note 64, above), His successor Constans also provided for the annual cost of the grain supply to Athens: Eunapius, *Vita Soph.*, 492.

[68] It cannot be proven that Athens was totally dependent on the emperor for her grain supply. Even if she did obtain much of it through her own initiative, however, she was vulnerable, because Gothic incursions into Pontus would have severely damaged the only grain source available.

Thus the risky business of cultivating grain crops in Attica again became vital to the citizenry. Just as in pre-Solonian times, people turned their attention to the sky and rainfall. It should not be surprising to discover that that attention expressed itself religiously in a familiar form. Hymettos was still regarded as a weather mountain, and the altar of Zeus was remembered. With good reason, then, citizens would take themselves up to the mountain top to pray for rain. Most of the Roman lamps found in the Hymettos excavation belong to the end of the 4th and beginning of the 5th centuries after Christ, the very time when the Eastern Empire was facing so many troubles and Athens was not receiving grain from overseas. The lamps may well be connected with this predicament and represent pagan offerings for rain.[69]

The lamps reveal only a brief period of activity on Hymettos. But whether offerings ceased because foreign grain shipments were resumed or for some other reason is not known. It does seem reasonable to suppose that after Arcadius died, and order was re-established in the Eastern Empire, generous annual gifts of grain were once again presented to Athens.[70]

Whatever the reasons for its final abandonment,[71] this little rural shrine of Zeus is of no small interest, reflecting as it surely must the religious outlook of a segment of the Attic citizenry regarding the food supply. Founded initially when rain was all-important for the crops, the sanctuary was visited regularly until the conversion of the rural Attic economy and the establishment of the overseas grain trade. An almost complete hiatus of activity at the sanctuary lasting some ten centuries mattered little when at the end of the 4th century after Christ circumstances may have led to a situation similar to that of the pre-Solonian era. As Attic soil was again responsible for producing an adequate grain supply, so worshippers turned again to the weather mountain Hymettos.

---

[69] They are this rather than an early expression of Christian worship on a mountain. Paganism remained especially strong in Athens during the Late Empire (cf. Alison Frantz, *Dumbarton Oaks Papers* XIX, 1965, pp. 187-205), and pagan worship on Hymettos in the 5th century after Christ would not have been out of place. Pagans also seem to have kept alive the worship of Zeus on Mount Olympos into the Late Roman period, as shown by excavations on one of the mountain's peaks: cf. V. Kyriazopoulos and G. Libadas, Δελτ. 22, 1967, Μελεταί, pp. 6-14.

[70] The emperors who succeeded Arcadius seem to have been even more well disposed to Greece than those who preceded him. Constantinople, which was entirely a Latin city in conception and during its early history, began, with Arcadius, to become Hellenized: cf. A. H. M. Jones, *Dumbarton Oaks Papers* XVII, 1963, p. 14. The atmosphere was never more favorable for Athens to receive a dole of grain from the emperor.

[71] In my opinion it was the spread of Christianity which led to the abandonment of the altar. In subsequent periods of food shortage in Athens, Christians prayed for rain, but not yet on mountain tops. When they did begin building chapels on the summits of mountains, Hymettos was not favored with one.

APPENDIX A

OTHER DEITIES WORSHIPPED ON MOUNT HYMETTOS

Zeus Ombrios was not the only divinity worshipped on Mount Hymettos in antiquity. Zeus in other aspects and other deities also received offerings on the mountain. In what follows the evidence relating to these deities is briefly considered.[1]

ZEUS HYMETTIOS

Pausanias (I, 32, 2) notes a statue of Zeus Hymettios on Hymettos, but without stating where it was located. It quite likely stood near the excavated altar of Zeus and represented the second stage in the evolution of the sanctuary, the dedication of an image of the god.[2] A hard white limestone stele found in the hollow is probably the pedestal for the statue, a small bronze figure as indicated by cuttings on the stele's top surface. The stele was measured as being 1.95 m. tall by 0.24 m. thick. On the smooth front side were the slight traces of a four-line inscription of which the excavators could not make out a single letter. Young dated the stele to the late Archaic or early Classical period on the basis of workmanship.[3]

The erection of the statue of Zeus came at a time which saw the altar of Zeus almost completely abandoned. Some pottery and other artifacts of the Classical, Hellenistic, and early Roman periods were found in the hollow, but they attest only occasional visits, not regular use. The statue of Zeus Hymettios was a modest commemorative dedication, put up by devotees to preserve the memory of Zeus on the mountain top at a time when the altar was not being visited regularly.

It is doubtful that recognition was extended to Zeus Hymettios anywhere but on the summit of Hymettos.[4] J. N. Svoronos believed otherwise. He contended that both Zeus Hymettios and Zeus Ombrios were worshipped in Athens at the Kallirrhoe spring on the south bank of the Ilissos,[5] a stream which begins on the west slope of Hymettos and from which Athens drew much of its water. He claimed to have

---

[1] The worship places of two deities on Mount Hymettos are not discussed here: a sacred cave of Pan on the eastern slope above ancient Paiania, cf. E. Vanderpool, *A.J.A.* 71, 1967, pp. 309-311; and a sanctuary of Aphrodite near the sacred spring just above Kaisariani monastery, cf. Photios, *s.v.* Κυλλοῦ πῆραν.

[2] See Cook, *Zeus* I, p. 121.

[3] The stele is briefly mentioned and illustrated in *A.J.A.* 44, 1940, pp. 4-5. It was too heavy to be transported down the mountain and was reburied in the hollow by the excavators. I searched for it but was unable to find it.

[4] Of the lexicographers only Hesychios mentions him: *s.v.* Ὑμήττιος· Ζεὺς παρὰ Ἀττικοῖς.

[5] *Journ. intern. num.* 18, 1916-1917, pp. 34-36.

found evidence for this worship in a series of reliefs unearthed at the spring in which he thought Zeus Hymettios and Zeus Ombrios were depicted. These identifications are highly conjectural, however, and the reliefs have been given a much more likely interpretation as representing Zeus Meilichios and a chthonic cult.[6] Thus, in view of the absence of any less equivocal evidence, we are not justified in identifying a sanctuary of Zeus Hymettios on the bank of the Ilissos river in Athens.

Zeus Hymettios has long figured erroneously in another instance, the text of *I.G.*, II², 1035, an inscription which deals with the restoration and purification of state sanctuaries and properties in Attica during the early part of the first century after Christ. Tsountas, the original editor of the inscription, read Διὶ ['Τμητ]τίωι in line 55.[7] If this reading could stand, it would have important bearing on our sanctuary. However, a new study of the inscription now shows that what had previously been read as the two taus of Hymettios is definitely a pi, which obliges us to restore Διὶ ['Ολυμ]πίωι.[8]

Gaia

What is possibly a form of Gaia's name is scratched on a plate found at the sanctuary of Zeus on Hymettos (**10**). It would not be surprising to encounter her here, since as Earth she bore vegetation after receiving rain. The dedication could be a request made through Gaia to Zeus for rain. An interesting parallel to this stood on the Acropolis. Pausanias (I, 24, 3) mentions there a statue of Ge praying to Zeus for rain. It was probably located near the rupestral inscription of Ge Karpophoros which is cut in the rock just north of the Parthenon.[9]

Long ago C. H. Morgan argued vigorously against any connection between Zeus and Gaia with respect to prayers for rain.[10] But although neither the statue of Ge on the Acropolis nor the Hymettos dedication constitute proof that prayers for rain were normally offered to Zeus through the Earth Goddess, the supposition that this was sometimes the case is indicated.

Herakles

The poorly preserved foundation 31 meters north of the altar of Zeus was

---

[6] Cook, *Zeus* II, Appendix, M, pp. 1115-1119.

[7] Ἐφ. Ἀρχ., 1884, cols. 167-170.

[8] Despite the loss of Zeus Hymettios this decree did apparently call for the restoration of at least one sacred precinct on Hymettos, in lines 48-49. See now G. R. Culley, *Hesperia* 44, 1975, pp. 207-223, especially pp. 214 and 216.

[9] *I.G.* II², 4758. Inscription and statue have long been placed together: Frazer, *Pausanias* II, p. 299; W. Judeich, *Topographie von Athen*, Munich, 1931, pp. 239-240; G. P. Stevens, *Hesperia*, Suppl. III, *The Setting of the Periclean Parthenon*, Princeton, 1940, p. 19.

[10] *T.A.P.A.* 32, 1901, pp. 91-94.

identified as an altar of Herakles on the evidence of two inscriptions which were found there, **9** and **173**.[11] Herakles was not normally worshipped on mountain tops, with the notable exception of his sanctuary on Mount Oite. That was a special case, however, since Oite was the death-place of Herakles, and a sanctuary was established there in his memory. It is interesting to note that Mount Oite was sacred to Zeus, but worship of the god and the hero were apparently unrelated to each other.[12]

The worship of Herakles on Mount Hymettos was likewise unconnected with Zeus. His altar is better understood when one recognizes his special place in Attic religion. He was given more attention in Attica than any other region of Greece. At many localities about the Attic countryside there existed small shrines dedicated to him.[13] The small altar on Hymettos reveals that such attention extended even to the top of at least one Attic mountain.

Apollo Proopsios

Pausanias (I, 32, 2) mentions an altar of Foreseeing Apollo on Hymettos, but its location is not known.[14] Presumably a high vantage point is required, because the epithet, when used of a deity worshipped on a mountain, must indicate his ability to oversee his domain rather than refer to any prophetic powers of looking into the future. Somewhere on the summit ridge would be a likely spot for the altar, but no remains have been found there which could be attributed to it.

Another possible location for the altar of Apollo is the Profitis Elias peak above Koropi. There, as we saw earlier, the altar of Zeus Ombrios was erroneously placed. Kotzias contended that this so-called altar, a rough rock construction lying approximately midway between the two temple foundations, served both Zeus and Apollo.[15] He believed that the καί....καί construction in Pausanias' account of the altars indicated that they were one and the same. The location would seem suitable for the altar of Apollo, but in the absence of any more positive evidence this identification must be regarded as very uncertain.

[11] C. Yavis, *Greek Altars,* St. Louis, 1949, p. 110, no. 4, believes that the foundation represents a low monumental altar such as would be suitable for Herakles.

[12] Zeus was worshipped on the summit of Oite: Sophokles, *Trachiniai,* 1191; Herakles was honored on a spur of the mountain. Excavations revealed the sanctuary of Herakles to have been active from Archaic to Roman times: M. Pappadakis, Δελτ. 5, 1919, Παράρτημα, pp. 25-33.

[13] Cf. Harpokration, *s.v.* Ἡράκλεια. For a good discussion of the place of Herakles in Attic religion, see Lewis Farnell, *Greek Hero Cults and Ideas of Immortality,* Oxford, 1921, pp. 107-111. Testimonia for the worship of Herakles in Attica are collected by S. Solders, *Die ausserstädtischen Kulte und die Einigung Attikas,* Lund, 1931, pp. 76-80. The most recent study of the hero in Attica: Susan Woodford, *Studies Presented to George M. A. Hanfmann,* Cambridge, Mass., 1971, pp. 211-225.

[14] This may be the altar which is mentioned by Hesychios, *s.v.* Ὑμήττης· ἐν Ὑμήττῃ ὁ Ἀπόλλων τιμώμενος.

[15] See Πρακτικά, 1949, pp. 57-58.

ZEUS EPAKRIOS

The *Etymologicum Magnum* (*s.v.* Ἐπάκριος Ζεύς) mentions an altar of this deity on Hymettos, and we learn from a recently published inscription that the residents of the deme of Erchia offered regular sacrifices to him there in the month of Thargelion.[16] His altar would have been situated on the summit or on a prominent point lower down,[17] but there is no compelling reason to believe in any connection between Zeus Epakrios and Zeus Ombrios or Zeus Hymettios. The Erchia inscription belongs to the 4th century B.C., when the altar of Zeus on the summit lay unused. Accordingly, we must look elsewhere for the altar of Zeus Epakrios.

[16] The sacrificial calendar of Erchia published by G. Daux, *B.C.H.* 87, 1963, pp. 603-634 = *S.E.G.* XXI, 541; the offering to Zeus Epakrios: col. E, lines 59 ff.

[17] Both the *Etymologicum Magnum* and Hesychios, *s.v.* Ἐπάκριος Ζεύς, specify that altars of Zeus Epakrios were located ἐπὶ τῶν ἄκρων τῶν ὀρῶν.

APPENDIX B

SOME MOUNTAIN-TOP SITES (Plate 1)

ATTICA

Mount Hymettos was not the only Attic mountain possessing monuments sacred to Zeus. Pausanias (I, 32, 2) mentions an altar of Zeus Ombrios and Zeus Apemios, another of Zeus Semaleos, and a statue of Zeus Parnethios on Mount Parnes, and a statue of Zeus Anchesmios on Mount Anchesmos. There is little other literary or epigraphical evidence for the worship of Zeus on the mountains of Attica, but remains have been found on several other peaks which may be connected with such activity. After a consideration of the peak sanctuaries mentioned by Pausanias, the evidence from some other Attic mountains will be examined.[1]

Mount Parnes

Pausanias informs us that Zeus Ombrios and Zeus Apemios (Averter of Ills) shared a common altar on Parnes. A likely candidate for this altar is a large ash deposit discovered and excavated in 1959 during construction of a military installation on the highest peak, Ozea (+ 1412 m.). No official report of the excavation appeared, but a newspaper account described a thick layer of ash 100 square meters in area and over two meters deep. The deposit was filled with burned animal bones, pottery ranging from the Early Geometric period down to Archaic times, including an especially large number of Corinthian aryballoi, some Roman lamps, fragments of bronze knives, pins, and shields, and around 3000 iron daggers.[2] No inscriptions are reported which might identify the site more closely, so it must remain only a possibility that it is the votive dump of the altar of Zeus Ombrios and Zeus Apemios mentioned by Pausanias. There are some interesting chronological similarities with the excavated site on Hymettos, although nothing comparable to the large number of Corinthian aryballoi and iron daggers from Parnes was found on Hymettos.

---

[1] The section on Attica owes much to an unpublished paper available in the library of the American School of Classical Studies at Athens, "A Survey of Mountain-top Sanctuaries in Attica," by Esther Smith and Harriet Lowry, *American School of Classical Studies at Athens, School Papers,* 1954. The paper is valuable in that it contains information about peaks which are no longer accessible because of military installations at their summits.

[2] For convenient summaries, see E. Vanderpool, *A.J.A.* 64, 1960, p. 269; G. Daux, *B.C.H.* 84, 1960, p. 658; M. S. F. Hood, *Arch. Reports for 1959-60,* p. 8; *Arch. Reports for 1960-61,* p. 5.

Perhaps they could be explained as votive offerings to Zeus Apemios, who is unknown elsewhere.[3]

A second altar of Zeus on Parnes was that of Zeus Semaleos. The statue of Parnethian Zeus may have stood near by and represented the second stage of his cult. A prime location for the altar would seem to be Harma (+ 867 m.), a height near Phyle some distance to the southwest of the highest peak of Parnes. Augurs looked to this place from Athens for the flash of lightning which was the sign for sending an offering to Delphi.[4] Also, weather signs were read from clouds there.[5] The seemingly obvious connection between Harma and Zeus Semaleos has long been recognized,[6] although the top of this height is a most unlikely looking place for an altar. There is little earth atop Harma, only rough and jagged sheets of rock forming a very uneven surface. Neither sherds nor cuttings in the rock offer themselves as evidence for a monument there. Alternatively we might place the altar near that of Zeus Ombrios.[7]

For the altar of Zeus Epakrios on Parnes we have no evidence.[8]

TOURKOVOUNI

Pausanias is the only ancient source mentioning Mount Anchesmos, stating that it was a small mountain in the vicinity of Athens with a statue of Zeus. There are numerous hills close to Athens, but one of the most conspicuous of them is Tourkovouni, a little to the northeast of the city, and it has most frequently been identified as ancient Anchesmos.[9] This identification is bolstered by the fact that on its northernmost peak (+ 302 m.) are the remains of a probable sacred precinct. The site was described by Wrede, who identified an altar surrounded by a circuit wall. He also noted good quantities of sherds, especially of the Geometric period.[10]

[3] Any explanation is better than that suggested in the newspaper account, that the daggers and shield fragments indicate that the site was a funeral pyre for warriors killed in battle, and the Corinthian aryballoi that the warriors were Corinthians or Megarians who invaded Attica in the period of the wars for Salamis.

[4] Strabo, IX, 2, 11.

[5] Theophrastos, de Signis Tempestatum 3, 47.

[6] C. Bursian, Geographie von Griechenland I, Leipzig, 1862, pp. 252-253; Frazer, Pausanias II, pp. 426-427.

[7] It is interesting to note that one of the preserved epithets of Zeus among the Hymettos votive inscriptions is " Semios ", which undoubtedly confers a meaning similar to " Semaleos ".

[8] Etymologicum Magnum, s.v. Ἐπάκριος Ζεύς.

[9] Cf. A. Milchhöfer, Text II, p. 19; Frazer, Pausanias II, pp. 427-428. Frazer goes too far in allowing the possibility that Mount Lykabettos may have been considered part of Anchesmos in ancient times, and suggesting that the statue of Zeus Anchesmios may have stood atop the former. Geologically Lykabettos and Tourkovouni are part of the same range, but in antiquity they were regarded as quite separate mountains.

[10] Attika, Athens, 1934, pp. 13, 29, and pl. 9, the only published photograph of the altar and circuit wall. The site is also briefly described by Sterling Dow, C.W. 35, 1941-1942, p. 106, and C. Yavis, Greek Altars, St. Louis, 1949, p. 101, no. 11.

The site has since been excavated, but no report has appeared. There is no clear evidence among the remains that a statue once stood here, but the so-called altar, a simple rectangular structure of rough stones, and the circuit wall around it are visible. Numbers of sherds belonging to plain Geometric and Subgeometric cups and skyphoi are strewn about the area.[11]

CENTRAL ATTICA

The greater part of this region is taken up by the Mesogeia, a large, fertile plain. It is bounded on three sides by mountains, Hymettos on the west, Pentelikon on the north, and Pani, Merenda, Charvati, and Perati on the south, and on the east by the sea. Pentelikon is the most extensive of these mountains and is composed of several separate peaks. On the highest peak (+ 1107 m.), which is now a forbidden military zone, Smith and Lowry report finding quantities of Classical sherds and tile fragments. This site is near the rock-hewn platform on which the statue of Athena mentioned by Pausanias (I, 32, 2) may have stood,[12] and it could perhaps be connected with it. There is no mention of any connection between this peak and Zeus.

The Mavrovounia are prominent subsidiary peaks to the east of the main peak. Megalo Mavrovouni, with its twin peaks, provides a good view of the plain of Marathon and the plain of Athens. On the northern of the twin peaks (+ 762 m.) I found some sherds and tile fragments just east of the modern survey marker. Here there is a patch of blackened earth containing numerous coarse-ware sherds and tile fragments and two or three early black-glazed sherds, probably of the 7th century B.C. No architectural features are to be seen. The southern peak of Megalo Mavrovouni (+ 781 m.) has no ancient remains. Mikro Mavrovouni (+ 676 m.), which lies some 2000 meters to the south, was searched by Smith and Lowry, but it yielded only a handful of sherds, a few with traces of dull black glaze.

Of the peaks bordering the Mesogeia on the south, Mount Pani (+ 635 m.) is the highest. Its summit is a large flat area which provides a good view of the plain. A modern survey marker crowns the highest point, and at two places near it were found concentrations of sherds. The first is about 50 meters north of the marker and at roughly the same elevation. The spot is marked by a tumble of rocks around which can be picked up many fragments of plain and decorated Geometric and Subgeometric cups and skyphoi and splinters of burned animal bones. Twenty meters north of this, at a slightly lower level, occurs a similar concentration of sherds and bones. Here Smith and Lowry found two graffito sherds,[13] fragments of the

---

[11] It is doubtful that Pausanias actually visited any of the mountain-top sanctuaries which he mentions in our now familiar passage. He could easily have failed to mention an altar on Anchesmos had he not seen the place himself.

[12] Cf. Frazer, *Pausanias* II, p. 420.

[13] E. Smith and H. Lowry, *op. cit.* (note 1, above, p. 100), p. 25, fig. 2. The inscribed sherds

same types of Subgeometric cups which on Hymettos were frequently found to have inscriptions. One of these graffiti is an incomplete abecedarium preserving the first two letters of the alphabet. A plausible interpretation of the site would be to see the tumble of stones as the remains of a rough altar and the area to the north of this perhaps as a votive dump.

The ridge forming the top of Mount Merenda (+ 612 m.) is a distinctive feature of the central Attic skyline. The summit is a large, uneven plateau. At a point 20 meters west of the modern survey marker is a hole filled with loose earth and rocks, possibly enclosed by a wall of rough stones one meter on a side, although this is far from certain. Within the enclosure many small bits of pottery and burned bone are strewn about. I found several nicely decorated Geometric and Proto-attic pieces, as well as plentiful fragments of plain Subgeometric cups. This may be the site of another small peak altar.

The lower peaks of Charvati (+ 394 m.) and Perati (+ 308 m.) complete the chain of mountains along the south and southeast sides of the Mesogeia. I could find no traces of antiquity on either peak, although Smith and Lowry report a tumble of rocks at the summit of Charvati, including a possible foundation course bedded in the earth. They found only three pieces of pottery, fragments of black glaze.

SOUTHERN ATTICA

Cultivable land is much less plentiful south of the Mesogeia. The small plain of Anavyssos is the principle agricultural district of the area, while much of the rest is occupied by wooded hills. Keratovouni (+ 650 m.) is the highest peak in southern Attica. It is part of the same massif as Pani but properly belongs here. I was not able to visit the summit, which is now a military zone, but from high up the northern slope central Attica appears distant, and the greater part of the Mesogeia is cut off from view by Merenda. From the southern slope, on the other hand, no height rises to block the sweeping panorama which one enjoys of all of southern Attica. The plain of Anavyssos lies at one's feet, and the prominent hills of Lavreotiki can be seen clearly. Smith and Lowry visited the site before it was expropriated, and they discovered great quantities of sherds on the bare, rocky top. The sherds were mostly from the usual types of simple Geometric and Subgeometric cups and skyphoi, but there were also numerous fragments of coarse ware. No traces of a stone pile or burned bone are mentioned, but otherwise the site resembles those on Pani and Merenda.

Attic Olympos (+ 468 m.) rises steeply to the west of the plain of Anavyssos. Around the modern survey marker at the summit I found several fragments of good

and other material collected by Smith and Lowry from various peaks were put into the sherd collection of the American School in 1954.

black glaze and Megarian bowls. Smith and Lowry found an almost complete Megarian bowl here. The spot was greatly disturbed by emplacement of the marker, but a mass of stone rubble now scattered about it could be the remains of some rough construction. It is possible that some later sanctuary occupied this peak, but Eugene Vanderpool has made a much better suggestion to me. The summit of Olympos provides an excellent view of the southwest Attic coast, and at the same time is intervisible with a watchtower on a northern spur of Hymettos.[14] Thus, Olympos would have made an ideal location for a signal station. Without more evidence, however, the identification of the rubble on Olympos as a tower can remain only a conjecture.

Numerous hills occupy the rest of southern Attica. In the mining district I visited the peaks of Megalo Rimbari (+ 372 m.), Mikro Rimbari (+ 331 m.), Megali Vigla (+ 259 m.), and Mont Michel (+ 225 m.) but found no evidence for sanctuaries.[15] Smith and Lowry report the same for the unnamed peak (+ 360 m.) northeast of the modern mining settlement of Plaka.

West of the mining district Mount Profitis Elias (+ 356 m.) predominates. It overlooks the only cultivable plains south of Anavyssos, Kataphygi to the north and Photini to the south. The small, flat summit is crowned by a modern chapel of Profitis Elias. The earth around the chapel is very hard packed and shows no signs of burning. It was only on my second visit to this peak that I found some potsherds: fragments of two Protocorinthian aryballoi, several Phaleron cup fragments, and some 6th century black glaze. This could possibly be the site of another small peak altar, and more pottery could perhaps be found by excavation.

NORTHERN ATTICA

Defined for our purposes as the area east of Parnes and north of Pentelikon, this mountainous district offers many possible locations for mountain-top altars.

Immediately north of Pentelikon lies Stamatovouni or Dionysovouni (+ 650 m.) with a view north over low, wooded hills and the small plain of Koukounarti where the Marathonian Tetrapolis sacrificial calendar was found. There are traces of what may have been an ancient farmstead down the northern slope, but there are no remains on the summit.

A number of peaks border the landward sides of the plain of Marathon. Neither of the highest peaks, Aphorismos (+ 572 m.) and Agrieliki (+ 557 m.), yield any evidence of antiquity, but a prominent lower outcropping (+ 361 m.) on the eastern slope of the latter does. Here Soteriades found the rubble of a possible ruined altar and an ash deposit with burnt animal bones and a large amount of pottery, the latter

---

[14] The Hymettos tower is described by J. R. McCredie, *Fortified Camps*, pp. 117-119.

[15] The peak of Megalo (or Vigla) Rimbari is fortified with a rubble defense wall: cf. J. R. McCredie, *Fortified Camps*, pp. 75-77.

said to be mostly Geometric but ranging through the entire first millennium B.C.[16] Pottery can still be picked up today at the site in the interstices of the bare, jagged rock. Most of the fragments I found were from the same types of simple Geometric and Subgeometric vessels as were found at the Hymettos sanctuary.

To the north of the plain stretches the long ridge of Stavrokoraki. At its western end (+ 310 m.) are the foundations of a round tower. The location is superb for a watchtower, with good views of the northern part of the plain of Marathon and the hill country to the north. The spot produced only one diagnostic potsherd, a fragment of a 4th century black-glazed kantharos.

North of Marathon the primary cultivable district is the plain of Aphidna. It is not hemmed in by mountains, as the Mesogeia and plain of Marathon are, but is defined by low, rolling hills and some higher peaks. Beletsi (+ 840 m.), or Phelleus on some early maps, dominates the area. Its bare gray summit has remains of a substantial enclosure, probably a rubble fort.[17] It yields great quantities of roof tiles, coarse ware and some Classical or Hellenistic black-glazed fragments, but no earlier pottery or burnt animal bones.

To the north of this district are numerous peaks. I visited only one, Mavrenora (+ 647 m.), but found no traces of antiquity. A nearby peak to the east, Mavrovouni (+ 648 m.), lies within the confines of a military base and cannot be visited. Smith and Lowry did investigate Stravaëtos (+ 591 m.), a southern extension of Mavrovouni, but their search turned up nothing.

WESTERN ATTICA

Two of the main peaks west of Athens, Mount Skaramanga or Korydallos (+ 468 m.) and Mount Aigaleos (+ 453 m.), are now inaccessible due to military installations on their summits. I was unable to find any description of the summit of Skaramanga, which is today considered the southern half of Aigaleos, and I know of only one ancient site on the mountain, the remains of a heroon on the eastern slope.[18] Aigaleos, on the other hand, has been well explored and described. No votive remains are reported, but Smith and Lowry identified as many as seven ancient towers along the summit ridge. Most of these structures, however, have been shown to be rubble cairns or enclosures of indefinite date.[19]

West of Eleusis rises the distinctive outline of Mount Kerata or Trikeri. Its highest peak (+ 470 m.) has remains of antiquity: a rock-cut platform and cuttings

---

[16] Brief mention of the site can be found in Πρακτικά, 1935, pp. 154-155.

[17] For a recent description of the remains on Beletsi, see Y. Garlan, *Rev. Arch.*, Ser. 8, 1967, p. 293.

[18] Cf. A. Milchhöfer, *Text* II, pp. 12-14.

[39] See *B.S.A.* 52, 1957, p. 175, where only two of the structures are called towers. McCredie, *Fortified Camps*, p. 119, describes the tower on the highest part of the mountain.

to indicate some sort of enclosure, plus numerous fragments of Late Roman lamps and pieces of tile.[20] The lamp and tile fragments are especially thick on the north and south slopes and have evidently washed down from the area of the rock-cut platform. Though badly fragmented, some of the lamps could be dated, all to after the second half of the 5th century after Christ. A possible explanation might be to see this as the site of a small Christian shrine.

We possess sufficient data from the peak sanctuaries named by Pausanias, those on Hymettos, Parnes, and Anchesmos, to enable us to identify other shrines on Attic mountains. We may, accordingly, label the remains on Pani, Keratovouni, Merenda, Profitis Elias, and Agrieliki as peak sanctuaries.[21] The occurrence, in large numbers, of the same types of cups and skyphoi, pieces of burned animal bones, and deposits of ash are features common to these sites. The implication is that we are dealing with local sanctuaries of Zeus. Especially significant is the chronological correspondence of these sites, with the 8th and 7th centuries B.C. the best represented by pottery. Reason has been shown why the Hymettos sanctuary flourished during these centuries, and the same could hold true for other peak sanctuaries in Attica as well. Since grain crops were the principal cultivated items at this time, the inhabitants of every agricultural district would have concerned themselves with the rain god on a nearby mountain top.

These peak sites show a geographical distribution which adds further support to the contention that they pertain to agriculture and the rain god. All of them provide an excellent view and convey a sense of intimate connection with some agricultural district: the sanctuaries of Zeus on Hymettos, Parnes, and Tourkovouni (Anchesmos) go naturally with the Athenian plain, the sites on Pani and Merenda go with the Mesogeia, the site on Keratovouni with the plain of Anavyssos, that on Profitis Elias with the Photini plain, and that on Agrieliki with the plain of Marathon. If the locations of peak sites do have some meaning in this regard, it might explain the absence of peak sites in southeastern Attica, where agriculture was less important in ancient times, but would fail to account for their absence from northern Attica, especialy around the plain of Aphidna. It is worth noting that, unlike the sites on the summits of Hymettos, Parnes, and Anchesmos, none of those on other Attic peaks evolved beyond the first stage of mountain-top sanctuary or was remembered by later writers. It is probably because the altars on the three peaks near Athens served a larger number of townsmen that they possessed greater importance than the more strictly rural peak altars which were allowed to pass out of existence at an earlier stage of development.

[20] For the most recent description of this site, see V. Scully, *The Earth, the Temple, and the Gods,* New Haven and London, 1962, p. 135.

[21] The other frequent occupier of Attic peaks, the military outpost or watchtower, usually leaves some architectural remains and yields coarse, domestic pottery, in contrast to sanctuary sites with their quantities of painted pottery and usual absence of architectural features.

OTHER AREAS

I have made no attempt to investigate all of the mountain-top sanctuaries of Zeus mentioned in ancient literary sources, nor to survey thoroughly the peaks of any region besides Attica. I have on occasion climbed particular mountains in pursuit of whatever evidence their summits might yield, and although the data obtained from these efforts represent no systematic investigation, it seems worth while to record my findings, along with new information reported by other investigators for some other Greek peaks.

MOUNT APESAS

To the north of ancient Nemea rises this table-topped mountain ($+ 873$ m.) where Perseus is said to have sacrificed to Zeus Apesantios.[22] There is no explicit ancient reference to an altar of Zeus on the summit, but there are traces which indicate one. The summit is a spacious area dipping from east to west, with an uneven surface of bare rock and dense scrub oak. At the eastern end, around a modern survey marker, is a clear patch of burnt earth with potsherds and fragments of bone.[23] The sherds are mostly of recognizable Corinthian fabric, Late Geometric and 7th century in date, with a few later black-glazed pieces. No construction is discernible, but loose rubble is especially thick in the area and could be the tumble of a rubble altar.

MOUNT ARACHNAION

This complex is located to the northwest of the sanctuary of Asklepios at Epidauros. Its sides are bleak and devoid of vegetation, but from a distance certain veins of rock outcropping give the appearance of confused spider webbing, hence the mountain's name. Pausanias (II, 25, 10) states that Zeus and Hera each had an altar on Arachnaion at which people offered sacrifices for rain. We are not told exactly where the altars were located, but they have long been associated with some remains in the saddle between the two highest peaks, Profitis Elias and Mavrovouni. The saddle is high and spacious and contains a large outcropping of limestone which is enclosed on the north, east, and west sides by rubble walls, in places preserved to a height of four meters.[24] On the south the outcropping falls away sharply and is

[22] Pausanias, II, 15, 3.

[23] For a description of the mountain and this site, see Ernst Meyer, *Peloponnesische Wanderungen*, Zurich and Leipzig, 1939, pp. 16-18.

[24] It appears that Boblaye was the only explorer to visit the site and give a first-hand description of the remains. Subsequent travelers all copy him. Boblaye called the enclosure in the saddle Cyclopean, which it definitely is not, and identified it as the spot where Zeus and Hera had their altars. For further references to other early travelers who mention the site, see Frazer, *Pausanias* III, pp. 233-234. Cook, *Zeus* II, p. 894, note 1 merely summarizes Frazer.

unwalled. Within, an area of approximately 75 by 20 paces, the earth is thick but unburnt. There are numerous coarse-ware sherds and obsidian chips to be found, but no other traces of antiquity. Clearly these scant remains do not support the placing in this area of the altars of Zeus and Hera.

Directly to the west of the saddle looms the highest peak of Arachnaion, Profitis Elias (+ 1199 m.). The summit is a small rounded top which affords a spectacular view of the entire Argolid but for the eastern coast. The foundations of two ancient structures are situated on the summit, but they are almost completely buried in the blackened earth which covers the top. Enough is visible, however, to allow a determination of their size and shape. Both are sizable rectangular constructions, one roughly 13 by 6 meters, the other 12 by 5 meters. The interiors of both have been dug out and are now filled with quantities of stone rubble. The walls average between 0.50 and 0.75 meters thick and are built of medium-sized limestone blocks with roughly smoothed outer faces. Potsherds abound over the whole top, with Late Geometric and 7th century pieces especially numerous. Some later black glaze is also present. Bone fragments also occur in quantities. This site with its two ancient foundations is a most suitable candidate for the altars of Zeus and Hera mentioned by Pausanias, and I feel confident that this identification is correct.

Mount Kokkygion

Cuckoo mountain, upon which Zeus had an altar,[25] is located in the southern Argolid just west of Hermioni. The mountain has two peaks, the northern one steep and barren and possessing a small chapel of Profitis Elias, the southern one rising more gently, with a substantial soil cover and heavy undergrowth. I undertook a search of both peaks but failed to uncover any trace of Zeus' altar.[26]

Mount Loutraki

T. J. Dunbabin reported a site on the bare pinnacle of limestone (+ 1069 m.) at the western end of the ridge of Mount Loutraki opposite Corinth.[27] He picked up Mycenaean, Protocorinthian or Corinthian, and Attic sherds on top of the outcrop and down its sides. John Pollard also visited the site and found some terracotta sima fragments and what he claims to be a small artificial platform.[28] It takes good will to see this platform. The top of the pinnacle is fairly flat, but this appears to

[25] Pausanias, II, 36, 2.
[26] M. H. Jameson had no better luck in a similar search in 1950, turning up only one black-glazed sherd near the chapel: V. B. and M. H. Jameson, "An Archaeological and Topographical Survey of the Hermionid," *American School of Classical Studies at Athens, School Papers,* 1950, pp. 45-46.
[27] *Perachora* I, pp. vii-viii.
[28] See *B.S.A.* 45, 1950, pp. 63-65, and *Greece and Rome*, N.S. 15, 1968, pp. 78-81.

be natural. Sherds are in evidence, as Dunbabin reported, but those I saw were so shattered and in such bad condition that dating them was impossible. I did find one diagnostic piece on the summit of the pinnacle, a fragment of a Mycenaean psi-type figurine.

From this peak the Isthmus of Corinth and much of the Corinthian and Saronic gulfs are visible. It is an ideal location for a military watchpost, but the remains do not suggest this. Instead, a small shrine, perhaps of Zeus or related to the nearby Heraion, may have been situated here.

Mount Kithairon

Pausanias not only informs us that Kithairon was sacred to Zeus (IX, 2, 4), but that the Plataians made offerings to Zeus and Hera at a wooden altar on the summit (IX, 3, 6-8). I know of no report of any antiquities on the summit (+ 1404 m.), nor was I able to carry out any investigations there due to the presence of a military installation.

Mount Helikon

Hesiod, *Theogony* 4 is the only literary reference to an altar of Zeus on Helikon. This altar has generally been identified with a rectangular construction, later converted into a chapel of Profitis Elias, on Zagaras, the easternmost peak of Helikon (+ 1526 m.; this peak is just off the upper edge of the map, Plate 1, toward the left). The structure measures ten by five meters and its walls are of loose polygonal construction, 1.35 meters thick. Numerous glazed roof tiles, potsherds (predominantly from 6th and 5th century black-glazed cups), and bits of burned bone can be picked up in and around it. The identification of this structure as the altar of Zeus does present problems. With its rather spacious dimensions and thick walls, it offers a sharp contrast to the securely identified mountain-top altars of Zeus which are distinctive in their simplicity. The building on Helikon might instead have served a military function, as a watchpost. The summit does offer a commanding view over a large area of southern Boiotia and the Gulf of Corinth, and the large number of ancient tiles suggests a roofed building and the housing of men rather than a simple open-air altar.

Recently, Paul W. Wallace came to the same conclusion regarding the structure and rejected completely its identification as the altar of Zeus.[29] There is, however, one piece of evidence not considered by Wallace which does confirm that this peak

---

[29] *Gr. Rom. Byz. St.* 15, 1974, pp. 23-24. One of Wallace's objections to the identification may be easily dispensed with. In remarking that the ancient structure was converted into a chapel of Profitis Elias, Wallace claims that Helios was generally the predecessor of Elias at places showing religious survival. Cook's discussion, *Zeus* I, pp. 163-186, should quiet any uneasiness on that score. Both Zeus and Helios were succeeded by the prophet and the former case was far too common a phenomenon to allow for any surprise or objections.

of Helikon was a sacred place. A rim fragment of an Archaic bronze lebes in the National Museum at Athens, and bearing a dedicatory inscription, is said to have come from Zagaras.[30] The inscription is fragmentary, so the restoration $[--\dot{\epsilon}]\mu\grave{\iota}$ τô 'Ελιϙον[ίο Διός --] can only remain a tempting conjecture. Plassart rejected it, since Helikonios is nowhere attested as an epithet of Zeus. Poseidon is the only deity called Helikonios [31] and Plassart would favor him as the recipient of the inscribed lebes. This certainly remains a possibility, but Plassart's argument against restoring Zeus as the deity is not strong. As we have seen in many other cases, Zeus was often named after a particular mountain on which he was worshipped. We have no good reason to believe that the same would not hold true for Mount Helikon, and it is quite probable that Zeus was worshipped as Zeus Helikonios there. I am inclined to accept the lebes as a dedication to Zeus and, despite the presence of ancient roof tiles, to identify the site on Zagaras as the altar of Zeus,[32] while at the same time recognizing that the identification can be disputed and must in fact remain an open question.

MOUNT OCHE

This Euboian mountain ($+ 1475$ m.) occupies the southern end of the island. Its most famous antiquity, the so-called Dragon House, lies near the summit. The building has been investigated, and numerous finds of pottery, ash, and burned bone are reported, especially from under the floor.[33] In a cavity of rock outside the Dragon House was found a cache of Archaic sherds, some of them inscribed. These finds are not fully published but they do suggest that before construction of the Dragon House a small sanctuary existed on the peak.

MOUNT OLYMPOS

During construction of a weather station on the peak of Ayios Antonios ($+ 2817$ m.) in the central cluster of the mountain a layer of burned earth containing

[30] Published by A. Plassart, *B.C.H.* 50, 1926, pp. 385-387; for better readings, see Jeffery, *L.S.A.G.*, p. 91, discussion of no. 6.

[31] *Iliad* XX, 404. The derivation of this title of Poseidon has been a matter of dispute, but it seems more likely that it stems from Helikon in Boiotia than Helike in Achaia; see on this M. Nilsson, *Griechische Feste*, Leipzig, 1906, p. 75, note 1. Poseidon Helikonios crops up later in Asia Minor: F. Sokolowski, *Lois sacrées de l'Asie Mineure*, Paris, 1955, no. 1, line 2, a decree of Sinope, 3rd century B.C.

[32] I am not so much bothered by the unsuitability of the structure on Zagaras as an altar of Zeus as I am by the silence of Pausanias. We must remember that we are dealing with a structure that was converted into a Christian chapel, so we cannot be certain of its original form or even, without excavation, ascertain which blocks are *in situ*. Pausanias' silence is by no means fatal, but it is bothersome that he has not a word to say about an altar of Zeus on Helikon, whereas he is conscientious in noting venerable altars of Zeus on other mountain peaks in Greece.

[33] N. K. Moutsopoulos, Τὸ Βουνό 217, 1960, pp. 147-163.

bone fragments and a number of antiquities was exposed.[34] The pottery from this deposit was mainly Hellenistic, with some Roman, while the coins found date from the mid-4th to the mid-5th centuries after Christ. That this peak was the site of a sanctuary of Zeus is proven by three stone dedications to Zeus Olympios also found in the burnt layer. This is the only peak of Olympos which has been investigated archaeologically, so the possibility of an earlier sanctuary of Zeus somewhere else on the mountain complex cannot be ruled out.

Mount Zevs

This mountain (+ 1003 m.) is located in the southern part of Naxos and is the highest in the Cyclades. It was called "Mountain of Zeus Melosios" in antiquity, as is revealed by a rupestral inscription on the mountain's western slope,[35] and the name "Zevs" appears to be a direct survival.[36] An ancient altar of Zeus at the summit would not be surprising, although none has ever been reported. In fact, a good candidate presents itself quite near the highest point. About 35 meters north of the modern survey marker is a flat area with a deposit of blackened soil containing a large amount of burned bones and potsherds. Most of the sherds are small and undiagnostic. They are coated with dull, streaky brown or black glaze and belong to simple open shapes which I would assign to the 7th or 6th century B.C.[37] There is no evidence of a structure, but it is quite possible that the pottery and bone fragments represent offerings made at a small, rustic altar near the summit.

[34] V. Kyriazopoulos and G. Libadas, Δελτ. 22, 1967, Μελ., pp. 6-14.

[35] I.G., XII, 5, 48, 4th century B.C.

[36] Cook, Zeus I, p. 163, states that the ancient name of the mountain was Drios, citing Diodoros, V, 51, 4. But Diodoros does not give any details about the location of Mount Drios, and I can see no compelling reason for identifying it with Mount Zevs. I believe that Mount Zevs always bore the name "Zeus," although this is admittedly conjectural for the time before the rupestral inscription. Another rupestral inscription on the mountain, this one in Latin and of the 17th century after Christ, reveals the continuity of the name. It is carved on a slanting outcropping of bedrock 13 meters south of the modern survey marker. The letters are shallowly cut (letter height 0.03 m.) and many of them illegible. The following readings could probably be improved upon with more work:

> Ex hoc vertige
> montis Iovis
> Melosii maris
> Aegæi circum..
> 5 .ASINSVIAS..N
> .ERABAT CAR....
> O.ERMAR..IO
> BENOINTEL....
> CALLIS......
> XXIV Nov MDCLXXIII

[37] The only securely datable piece from this deposit is a ray-base fragment of a 7th century B.C. Corinthian kotyle. This sherd was found by J. J. Coulton, to whom I am indebted for bringing to my attention the site on Mount Zevs.

The most interesting feature of the mountain-top sites discussed above is their chronological similarity. With the exception of the altar on Mount Olympos, the sanctuaries on Apesas, Arachnaion, Oche, and Zevs all flourished at the same time, the late 8th to 7th century B.C. This could possibly indicate some widespread development in Greek religion regarding Zeus. In this case the deity's worship on Attic peaks would have to be reconsidered, in view of the fact that Attic peak altars were most active at the same time as those in other areas. Until the commencement of more systematic research and excavation of mountain tops in these other areas, however, we are forced to consider each area separately and to formulate hypotheses based on local circumstances. Thus the Attic peak altars and their chronology become intelligible in the light of the situation there. Further speculation would be rash without more evidence. The purpose of this brief survey has been to draw attention to the remains of several interesting peak sites. Many of the peaks that I was able to investigate personally will no doubt eventually be expropriated and all evidence from them destroyed before proper excavations have a chance to better elucidate their nature.

INDICES

References to the catalogues are given in bold-faced numbers

ANCIENT AUTHORS

INSCRIPTIONS

GENERAL

PLATE 1

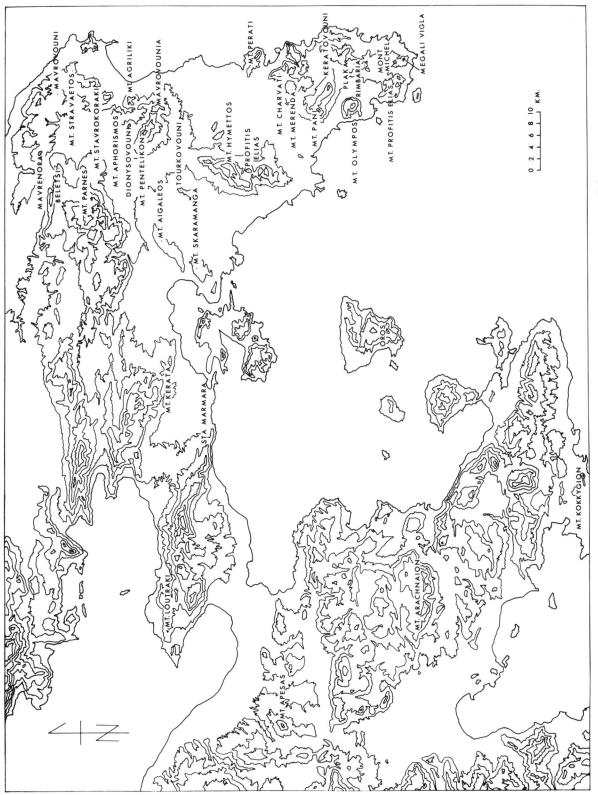

Map showing mountain tops explored in Attica, Corinthia and Argolid

PLATE 2

View in the hollow looking north, May 2, 1923

1

2

3

4

Scale 1:1

PLATE 3

5

6

7

8

9

11

14

15

16

17

18

Scale 1:1

PLATE 4

20

22

23

24

25

27

28

29 c, a, b

30

Scale 1:1

PLATE 5

31

32

33

34

35

38

40

41

42

Scale 1:1

PLATE 6

43 b

43 a

46

47

48

49

51

52

53

55

56

Scale 1 : 1

PLATE 7

57

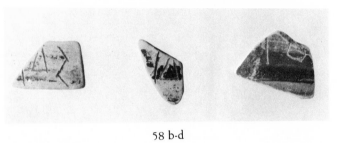

54

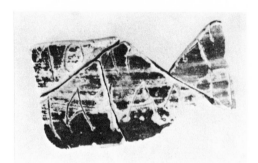

58 a

58 b-d

60

59 a : a, b; below, 59 b

65

67

Scale 1:1

PLATE 8

63 a-c

66 a, b

68

69

70

71

72 a, b

73

74

75

76

Scale 1:1

PLATE 9

78 a-c

79

80

81

82

83

84

85

86

87

88

89

PLATE 10

90

91

92

93

94

95

96

97

98

99

100

101

103

104

Scale 1:1

PLATE 11

105

106

107

109

110

111

112

113

114

115

116

117

118

120

121

Scale 1:1

PLATE 12

122

123

124

125

126

127

128

129

130

131

132

133

134

135

136

137

Scale 1:1

PLATE 13

138

139

140

141

142

143

144

145

146

147

148

149

150

151

152

Scale 1:1

PLATE 14

153 a   153 b   154 a   154 b

155

158

156 (2:1)

159   160

162   163

164

165

Scale 1:1 except 156

PLATE 15

166

167

168

169

170

171

172

173

Scale 1:1

PLATE 16

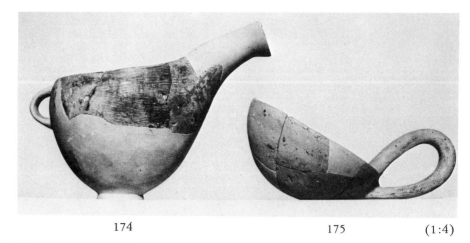

174   175   (1:4)

176   177   178

179   180

182

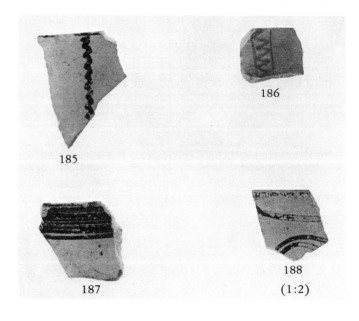

185   186

187   188

(1:2)

PLATE 17

183   181   184 (1:2)

189

190 (1:4)   191 (1:4)   192 (1:4)

193 (1:5)   194 (1:5)   195 (1:4)

196

PLATE 18

197   199   (1:5)   201   200   204 (1:4)

198   203   205 (1:4)   202 (1:4)

207   208   209 (1:4)

210   212   213 (1:4)

206   211

214   215 (1:4)

PLATE 19

216   217 (1:4)

218 (1:2)   219 (1:4)

220   221   222 (1:4)

223

224   225 (1:4)   227 (1:4)   228 (1:4)

229   233   230   231

PLATE 20

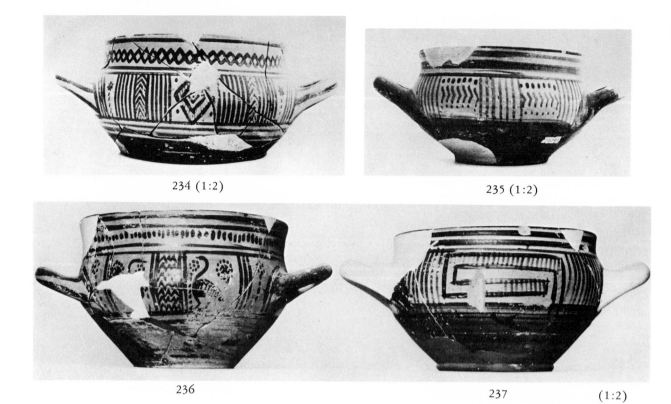

234 (1:2)

235 (1:2)

236

237   (1:2)

239

240 (1:3)

242 (1:2)

241

238

PLATE 21

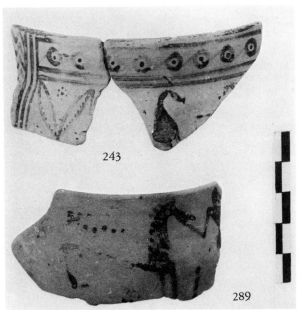

243

289

244

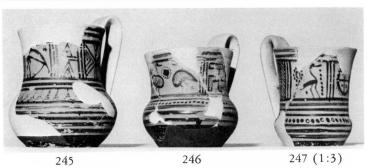

245   246   247 (1:3)

248 (1:3)

249 (1:3)

250 (1:3)

251   253 (1:4)

PLATE 22

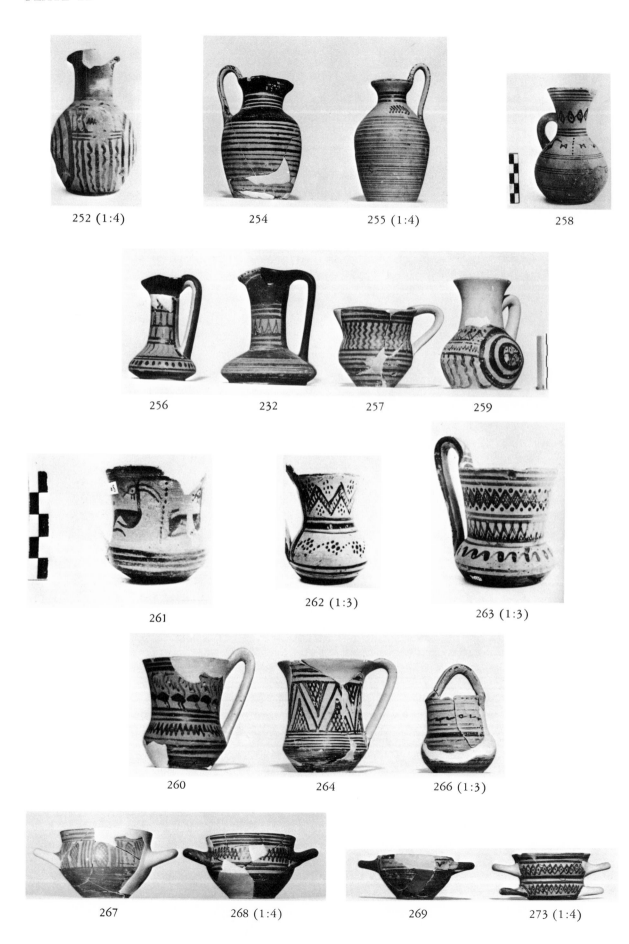

252 (1:4)   254   255 (1:4)   258

256   232   257   259

261   262 (1:3)   263 (1:3)

260   264   266 (1:3)

267   268 (1:4)   269   273 (1:4)

PLATE 23

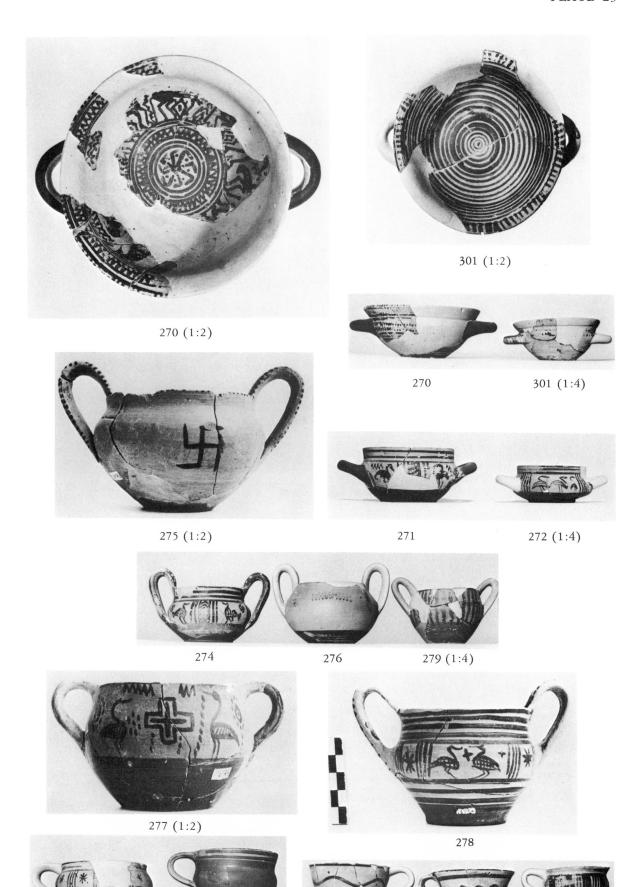

270 (1:2)

301 (1:2)

270   301 (1:4)

275 (1:2)

271   272 (1:4)

274   276   279 (1:4)

277 (1:2)

278

226   280 (1:4)

281   282   284 (1:4)

PLATE 24

283 (1:2)

286 (1:2)

285   287 (1:4)

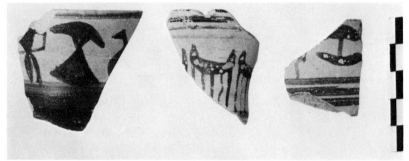

288   290   291

265   293   295 (1:2)

298

292   300   302 (1:4)

PLATE 25

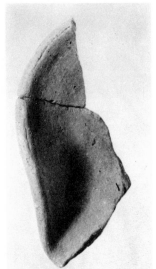

306 (5:6)

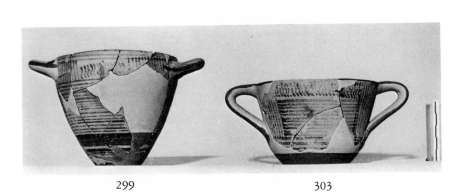

299 303

296 297 304

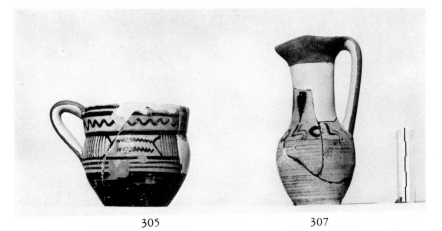

305 307

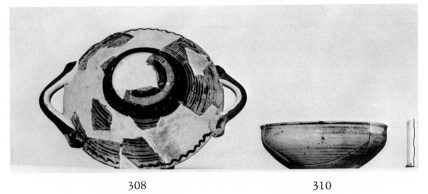

308 310

PLATE 26

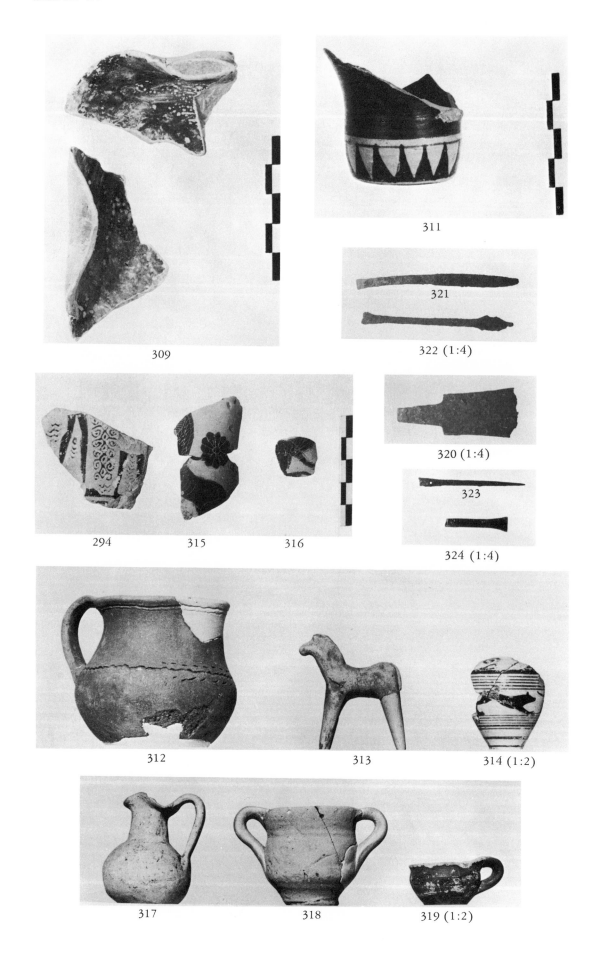

309

311

321

322 (1:4)

294   315   316

320 (1:4)

323

324 (1:4)

312   313   314 (1:2)

317   318   319 (1:2)

PLATE 27

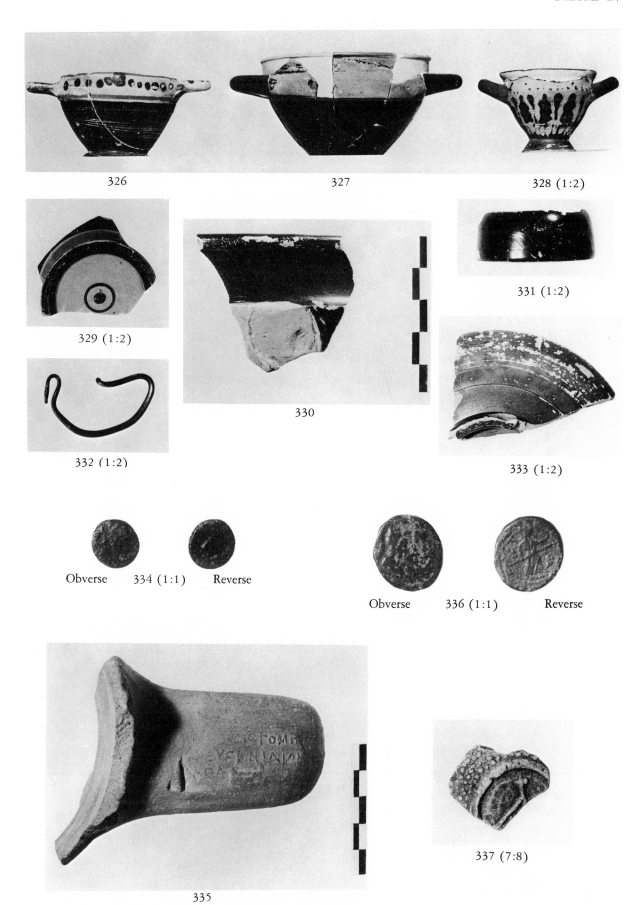

326

327

328 (1:2)

329 (1:2)

332 (1:2)

330

331 (1:2)

333 (1:2)

Obverse   334 (1:1)   Reverse

Obverse   336 (1:1)   Reverse

335

337 (7:8)

PLATE 28

Obverse   338 (1:1)   Reverse

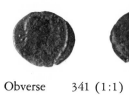

Obverse   341 (1:1)   Reverse

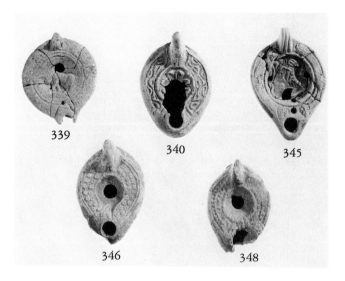

339   340   345

346   348

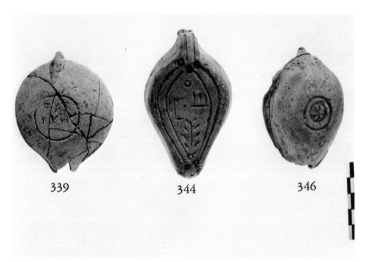

339   344   346

343

342   349